WALKING WITH
GOD

WALKING WITH GOD

LEARNING DISCIPLESHIP IN THE PSALMS

Richard D. Phillips

THE BANNER OF TRUTH TRUST

THE BANNER OF TRUTH TRUST
3 Murrayfield Road, Edinburgh EH12 6EL, UK
P O Box 621, Carlisle, PA 17013, USA

*

© Richard D. Phillips 2005
ISBN 0 85151 895 8

*

Typeset in 11/14 pt Sabon at
The Banner of Truth Trust
Edinburgh

*

Printed in the U.S.A.
by Versa Press, Inc.,
Peoria, IL

To My Beloved Mother
Proverbs 31:28

AND
To the Blessed Man
Jesus Christ
WHOSE LEAF IS
EVER GREEN

CONTENTS

PREFACE

No book of the Bible more directly connects with the life of faith than the Book of Psalms. Here we find recorded a whole range of human emotions and experiences common to the life of faith in a difficult and often hostile world, providing us with a handbook for Christian living that covers every topic in the curriculum. In a time like ours, when false spirituality abounds both within and without the church, the Book of Psalms is God's guide to true spirituality.

One significant difference between Christians today and the Christians of previous generations is our unfamiliarity with the psalms. The problem is not merely that we do not know more than a few psalms, but more profoundly, that we are not intimate with the spirituality that breathes through this most personal book of sacred Scripture. Our estrangement from God's handbook for the heart helps to account for the fact that so few Christians today walk closely with God.

One way for believers to improve their walk with the Lord is to commune with him through the psalms. Here, the Lord places his own words into the mouths of believers to help them call out to him. Here are songs of the heart that God teaches us to sing – songs of joy, songs of pain, songs of fear, and songs of faith. The psalms in laying bare the heart of true faith also connect us directly to the heart and song of our Lord Jesus Christ. While many of the psalms directly prophesy Jesus' experience in this world, all the psalms are his and are intended both to instruct the Christian's mind and shape his heart.

My own love affair with the psalms stems from a desire for a more lively prayer life. On the advice of a wise author, I began praying through the psalms and discovered that, by doing so, God himself was helping me to pray. I have also had the pleasure of witnessing the powerful impact of the psalms in my wife's experience. Through her own pursuit of the Lord in the psalms I have seen her knowledge of God increase and have heard her speak of the rich communion she has enjoyed with her Saviour. Experiencing such blessings on my family through the psalms, it was only natural that I wanted to preach on this matchless collection of biblical poetry in the hope that other Christians might be strengthened in their own walk with the Lord. It is my prayer that you will be drawn closer to God as you learn discipleship through the psalms. I further pray that if you are not familiar with the psalms you will find in this book a helpful introduction to this beautiful portion of Scripture.

I want to express my thanks to my wife, who is the helper of my heart and my close companion in walking with God. I praise God for the lessons he has taught to me simply by participating in her life. I am grateful to the Session and congregation of First Presbyterian Church of Coral Springs/Margate, Florida, where I serve as Senior Minister and to whom these chapters were delivered in sermon form. I also am grateful to the dear saints of Tenth Presbyterian Church in Philadelphia, Pennsylvania, to whom many of these messages were first delivered.

This book is dedicated to my mother, Margaret Phillips, for whom I give grateful thanks to God for the grace she so freely spreads and for her constant love and support. Finally, I give humble thanks to the Lord, for he is good, for his steadfast love endures forever!

RICHARD D. PHILLIPS
Coral Springs, Florida
Maundy Thursday, 2004

I

THE WAY OF BLESSING
PSALM 1

He is like a tree planted by streams of water that yields its fruit in its season and its leaf does not wither. In all that he does, he prospers (*Psa.* 1:3).

O ne of the most arresting statements in the New Testament was that made by our Lord Jesus Christ only minutes before his arrest. It is found in what is known as Christ's High Priestly prayer (*John* 17). In this prayer Jesus commits into the Father's hands the care of the disciples he is about to leave behind. In verse 1 he prays for God to glorify him because of the work he has completed, and in verse 2 he speaks to the Father of his own authority to grant eternal life. Then in verse 3, he makes the statement that defines the eternal life he supplies; this is what Christianity is all about. 'This is eternal life, that they know you the only true God, and Jesus Christ whom you have sent' (*John* 17:3).

Salvation – eternal life – consists of knowledge. This knowledge is not of things or even of doctrines, but of a Person; it is the personal knowledge that comes through a relationship with God and his Son, Jesus Christ. This is eternal life.

We are saved for communion with God. Yet this is something that many Christians struggle to realize. We know about God. We could answer questions about salvation and what it means to be saved. But when it comes to a real relationship, and to the experience of fellowship with God, that is something about which we are not so sure and confident.

There are two reasons for this, the first of which deals with the way we think about salvation. Most of our attention focuses on what we are saved *from* and the means by which we are saved. We are right to emphasize this because if, for instance, we get the doctrine of justification wrong (the Bible's teaching about how we are accepted by God), we are going to have terrible problems with the whole of the Christian life. Salvation from sin is the foundation of the Christian life, so we rightly emphasize this in our thinking. Nonetheless, it is not enough for us to be saved from sin, condemnation, and death; we are also saved *to* newness of life, and to fellowship with God.

The first reason for this problem, then, has to do with our thinking, but a greater reason has to do with ourselves, and with the reality of life in the here and now. We live in a fallen world of sin and weakness. Our sinful nature continues to war against the Spirit. Our spiritual vision is imperfect; we see as those gazing in a glass darkly. It is no surprise, then, that we need help in relating to the invisible God, in our communion with him, in walking with the God who is 'spirit'.

Yet, according to Jesus, salvation ultimately consists of this very thing – communion with God. Peter Lewis tells of a Chinese pastor who was imprisoned in a labour camp for his faith. His captors denied him a Bible and punished him when he prayed or sang. Out of their malice they made him clean the contents of the camp latrine. Every day he would take the foul excrement out and scatter it as fertilizer over the fields. The smell was so bad that the guards drew away and gave him plenty of space to do his foul work. But the persecuted pastor grew to love his lowly occupation for this very reason, because in the resulting solitude he could talk and sing to God to the satisfaction of his soul. The dunghill became his 'garden', and he sang:

> I come to the garden alone, while the dew is still on the roses . . .
> For he walks with me and he talks with me, and he tells me I am
> his own;
> And the joy we share as we tarry there, none other has ever
> known.[1]

That is what the Christian life is intended to be, abiding fellowship with our loving God no matter what the outward circumstances may be. The whole Bible is given to bring us into relationship with God, but the Book of Psalms especially takes us by the hand and leads us into living fellowship with him. If you desire to walk with God, to know him day to day and relate to him as he intends, to learn how to pray, then I can do no better than commend the Book of Psalms, the Bible's own book of personal communion with God.

The place to start the Book of Psalms is Psalm 1, which serves as a gateway for this whole collection of divinely inspired poetry. Psalm 1 presents a thesis that is developed in the rest of the book, namely, that there is a way of blessing open to those who trust in the Lord. Here is God's own philosophy of life for men and women.

We see this in the very first verse of the whole Psalter: 'Blessed is the man'. This is the quest of mankind – blessing. If you ask people what they are looking for they will speak of this very thing. They will say, 'I want to be happy.' It is not wrong to want this; according to the Bible, it was with blessing in mind that God created us in the beginning.

How wonderful this is, then, to hear from God that there is a way for blessing, fulfilment and satisfaction. This psalm gives us the hope the world has lost, namely, that happiness really is possible for us. This is what the Bible tells the world. We do not have to settle for grim despair; we don't have to choose between

---

[1] From Peter Lewis, *God's Hall of Fame* (Fearn, Ross-shire: Christian Focus, 1999), p. 32.

the way of the stoic or the way of the cynic. The aching longing of our hearts can be realized. We can be blessed.

The Two Ways

Everyone wants to be happy, but Psalm 1 shows us that the way we pursue happiness is all important. Verses 1–2 set out before us the two basic ways of seeking happiness, starting with the way the blessed man does not walk and then presenting the way that he does. This reminds us that the Christian gospel always involves both a negative and a positive message. That is something people do not like to hear today; they want Christianity to be positive only. But there are two ways, according to the Bible, and if we sincerely want to be blessed we must say 'No' to one and 'Yes' to the other. Jesus echoed this teaching when he said, 'For the gate is wide and the way is easy that leads to destruction, and those who enter by it are many. For the gate is narrow and the way is hard that leads to life, and those who find it are few' (*Matt.* 7:13–14).

First, the psalmist considers the broad way that leads to destruction. Many travel down this road, but not the blessed man; he avoids it, and walks a different way altogether. 'Blessed is the man who walks not in the counsel of the wicked, nor stands in the way of sinners, nor sits in the seat of scoffers' (verse 1).

What a detailed description of the godless life this verse supplies! Did you notice the definite progression contained within these words? First the person is *walking*, then *standing*, before finally *taking his seat* as he settles into the sinful life he has chosen for himself. This is the slippery slope of sin, a progression that leads to a settled godlessness. We might think of someone at a social gathering, who walks by a certain crowd. After a while he is seen standing among them, and finally he sits down at their table. This is how we progress in the way of sin.

Furthermore, there is a progression in the nature of sin's influence. First, there is *counsel*. This is advice and persuasion;

the way of sin begins with our minds coming under the influence of the world. Next it is a *way*. The ideas have taken root in the mind and now they bear fruit in behaviour and habits. Then, lastly, we have the *seat* of scoffers. Now the man is seated in depravity, his character has been warped and he is at rest and at home in this way of sin.

This progression is also seen in terms of the people involved. The word used for *wicked*, which comes first, speaks of those who fall short of what God intends. This is the worldly man or woman who leads a lower sort of life, who does not aspire or attain after higher virtues. Next comes the *sinner*, and this word describes the one who breaks God's commandments. First we see unworthy aspirations arising but now we have moved on into outright transgressions. Finally, we have *scoffers*, those in open rebellion against God, morality, piety, and decency, far removed from repentance and saving faith.

If you put all this together, you have the vortex of sin into which so many are irresistibly sucked. First, they are merely under a bad influence, then they are trying it out, and finally, they are confirmed and committed in iniquity. Charles Spurgeon said, 'At first they merely walk in the counsel of the careless and ungodly, who forget God – the evil is rather practical than habitual – but after that, they become habituated to evil, and they stand in the way of open sinners who wilfully violate God's commandments; and let alone, they go one step further, and become themselves pestilent teachers and tempters of others, and they sit in the seat of the scornful. They have taken their degree in vice, and as true Doctors of Damnation they are installed, and are looked up to by others as Masters in Belial.'[2]

Notice that all this begins when we give ourselves to the counsel of the world and its low views of life. It is impossible to overstate the importance of this. First, comes an attitude we pick up from others, a way of thinking, a way of looking at the

[2] C. H. Spurgeon, *A Treasury of David*, 3 vols. (Peabody, MA: Hendrickson, n.d.), vol. 1, pp. 1–2.

world and its ideas of happiness. Think of the ideas coming out of the universities, that there is no truth, no reality, no meaning, and most of all, no authority. Then there is Hollywood's enticing portrait of the happiness that comes by being free from shackles, by experimenting with new things, and particularly by immersing yourself in practices that were once considered shameful but are so no longer. The licentious life is portrayed as the way to have fun and be blessed. That is the counsel of the wicked and many choose to walk under its influence.

It was with wicked counsel that the devil brought sin into the world. Eve began listening to him and before long she was thinking like the devil; then she entered into the way of sin. Finally she had to sit in her state of depravity. That is how sin works. If you expose your mind to the depravity of this world with its messages and promises of pleasure, if you watch the television shows and read the lurid novels and fill your mind with the angry or sexually debauched songs of popular culture, then you will be pulled into the downward spiral described here.

Young people especially need to be warned to guard their heart and mind, particularly during their impressionable and formative years. However, we all need to heed this warning. We think we can toy with sin and dabble in worldliness, but we discover here that we cannot. Walking in the counsel of the wicked leads to standing in the way of sinners and ultimately, if unchecked, to sitting in the seat of mockers.

Blessed is the man or woman who does not go down this slippery slope of sin. In contrast, 'His delight is in the law of the LORD, and on his law he meditates day and night' (verse 2). Just as the way of sin begins with wicked counsel, so the way of blessing begins with the Word of God. The psalmist speaks of the Torah, 'the law of the LORD', but this can refer to all parts of Scripture. The blessed man is not someone who reads God's Word under compulsion, as a dreary chore; rather he delights in it and thinks seriously about it day and night. It is the Bible that gives him his philosophy, that shapes his thoughts and attitudes, that fills his heart with the beauty of God's character and saving plan, that renews his mind with its transforming influence. The blessed man or woman has fellowship with God all the time, by thinking about his Word, praying to him in accordance with Scripture, and interacting with his Lord in every situation.

There is no clearer sign of the new birth than a delight in God's Word. And no wonder, for to be born again is to have the Spirit of Christ within you, and if verse 2 describes anyone perfectly then it must be Jesus Christ. When tempted by the devil in the wilderness he replied, 'Man shall not live by bread alone, but by every word that comes from the mouth of God' (*Matt.* 4:4). Those who are led by the Spirit of Christ will love God's Word. They do not rebel against God's hard commands but approve of them and seek his grace to live them out in daily practice. Most of all, they delight in the knowledge of God that comes through his Word. That is their greatest treasure. The blessed man is a Bible man – a man of the Book. By God's Word he is led in the narrow path that leads to life.

Streams of Living Water

Verses 1 and 2 contrast the two different ways of living, before the psalm proceeds to describe their totally different results. First, verse 3 says of the blessed man, 'He is like a tree planted by streams of water that yields its fruit in its season, and its leaf does not wither. In all that he does, he prospers.'

Notice that this says nothing about circumstances. It doesn't say that if you follow God and the Bible nothing bad will happen to you. The psalm offers a blessed life, not a problem-free life. Christians will go through trials and experience hardship, and the Book of Psalms makes this vividly plain. Indeed, there are some trials that are peculiar to a Christian precisely because he is the one who knows what it means to fight against sin.

The blessedness of which this psalm speaks is more wonderful than merely having good circumstances. If you trust God and walk in his counsel you will be like a tree planted by a stream of water. A tree can stand up to storms; it lives for many years, growing tall and strong and bearing fruit. A Christian is firmly planted, not in the soil of this world or of outward circumstances, not in the security and comfort that come from good jobs or family relationships, or any worldly powers – all of which may betray us – but is planted in God and the soil of his unchanging character, drawing life from the living waters of the salvation he freely gives.

There are some who consider the statement of this psalm to be completely unrealistic. For instance, the liberal scholar Walter Brueggemann complains that many godly people are not blessed in this world. He comments, 'Only the very sheltered, innocent, and unperceptive could embrace such a naïve affirmation as that made in Psalm 1 . . . The simple affirmation of Psalm 1 is not adequate to lived experience.'[3] Obeying God does not necessarily lead to blessing, he says, and many who trust God are let down. How do we answer that?

The best people to answer such criticism are Christians who have suffered greatly but who testify to God's sustaining grace. I think of the story of Art Matthews and his family, who were the last missionaries to escape from China after the communist take-over. They lived in a single room with only a stool for furniture. All contact with outside friends and financial support was cut off. With only a small stove for heat they often shivered, and their food was reduced to a daily meal of rice cooked over burning manure that Art had gathered in the streets. All through this trial they trusted God, they spoke to him in prayer and strengthened themselves by his Word. After they escaped, they told their story, and the title of the book gives an answer to the doubters of Psalm 1. It was drawn from Jeremiah 17:7–8, which has the same idea. The book was entitled *Green Leaf in Drought Time*, and was their testimony to the fact that God's people do

[3] Walter Brueggemann, *The Psalms & the Life of Faith* (Minneapolis: Fortress, 1995), pp. 196–7.

not wither in the most barren circumstances of life, but persevere in the joy of their fellowship with him. 'Blessed is the man who trusts in the LORD', Jeremiah said. 'He will be like a tree planted by the water that sends out its roots by the stream. It does not fear when heat comes; its leaves are always green.'

This is what I mean by the importance of communion with God. It means to be connected to him as a tree reaches out with its roots to a nearby source of water. When trial comes you shed your tears on his shoulder and steady yourself with his hand. The temptations of success do not overcome you because your life is rooted in God and you desire to please him in all things. It means that when you are frightened or hurt, when you are assailed outwardly or shaken inwardly, you remember his Word and hear his voice, rely upon his love and drink from the rivers of heaven. That is how the blessed life is energized. By delighting in God's Word and meditating on it day and night you grow in this relationship as God's Word grows in you. You become like a tree planted by a stream, ever green and flowering.

The Hebrew word used in this verse for *streams* has the particular meaning of an irrigation canal. That is, it is a source of water that has specifically been dug and directed to the tree. What a lovely statement of God's faithfulness! Your salvation relies on his work; you simply reach out with the roots of faith. That is why a Christian blooms even in the most barren circumstances – the loss of a job, ongoing disappointment, physical handicap, material poverty or impending death – because God brings life-giving, joy-imparting, power-supplying water to him by the ministry of the Holy Spirit through the gospel.

What then is the blessed life? It is like a tree 'that yields its fruit in season, and its leaf does not wither. Whatever he does prospers.' The blessed life does not consist of money, fame, or comfort. It is fruitfulness – the fruit that springs from the knowledge of God. It is seen in a character that is conforming to his image and good works that are pleasing to God and wholesome for us. It is eternal life born in us, a life whose leaf never withers. 'Though outwardly we are wasting away', Paul writes, 'yet inwardly we are being renewed day by day' (2 *Cor.* 4:16). It is a life in which our witness and good works produce an eternal harvest; however small and futile they may seem in the eyes of the world, they prosper in the soil prepared and watered by God.

That is what it means to be blessed. It cannot be purchased with money, but the poorest Christian may know it to the full. It depends not on your bloodline, race, or education, but flows from God through faith in his Word. This is the blessed life and any of us may have it, in any circumstance, in clear skies or dark, to the glory of God and through the power of his grace. The great hymn-writer John Newton wrote of it in these stirring words:

> See! the streams of living waters,
>   Springing from eternal love,
> Well supply thy sons and daughters,
>   And all fear of want remove.
> Who can faint while such a river
>   Ever flows their thirst to assuage?
> Grace which, like the Lord, the Giver,
>   Never fails from age to age.

The Wicked Like Chaff

Verse 4 ushers in a great contrast: 'The wicked are not so, but are like chaff that the wind drives away'. Chaff is made up of the bits of stem and husk that attach to the wheat. A farmer tossed the threshed grain into the air so that the chaff would blow away in the wind while the weightier grain would fall to the ground. Those who follow the counsel of the wicked, walk in sin and sit with the mockers are like the chaff. For all the noise and show they make in this world, they are ultimately exposed as rootless, barren, fruitless, lifeless, and weightless husks. This is the inevitable end of the way of sin described in verse 1. The agricultural contrast here is absolute. The two different ways set forth in this psalm have opposite results; one is likened to a well-planted tree that blooms enduringly; the other is likened to chaff that blows away and is gone for ever.

Hollywood and the entertainment industry often propagates the counsel of the wicked, telling us that sin is the way to really live. But what we read about the lives of the rich and famous shows that this description of chaff fits them perfectly. Generally speaking, the movie stars lead lives of misery, bondage to drugs, failed relationships, destruction and ruin; several 'stars' have finished their days in poverty and obscurity. Let us never envy the ungodly, however much they seem to have! For despite all the world's propaganda the saying is true: 'The wages of sin is death' (*Rom.* 6:23).

That is simply the natural outworking of the way of sin, apart from God's judgment, but verses 5 and 6 tell us something more. In this life the wheat and chaff grow together. But there is a harvest at the end, when the two will be separated finally. The two ways of life lead to two very different destinies. 'The wicked will not stand in the judgment, nor sinners in the congregation of the righteous' (verse 5). The happiness of sin is fleeting at best and ultimately is cursed by the judgment of God. The blessed assembly of heaven is barred to the wicked and their way will perish: the loud music will fail, the pleasures of the flesh will turn to pain, and the shining lights will flicker into flames.

But 'the LORD knows the way of the righteous' (verse 6). 2 Chronicles 16:9 says, 'The eyes of the LORD range throughout the earth to strengthen those whose hearts are fully committed to him.' However hard your way, if God is watching over you it leads to blessing – this is the testimony of the whole Bible. If God sent his Son to die for your sin – the most costly thing he ever could do – you may be sure that he will do whatever else it takes to lead you into the blessing he has prepared for you.

The Blessed Man

What good news it is that there is a blessed way! But the bad news is that none of us really fits the blessed man's description. The reason why this way of sin resonates with us – this description of walking and standing and sitting – and why it is given more treatment here than the godly way – is that we are so familiar with it. Is it not true that we all have walked and stood and taken our seat in the way of sin? How, then, can we ever cross over on to the path of blessing?

The answer is that God sent his Son into the world to be this blessed man. How well this portrait describes Jesus! He delighted in God's law. He bore fruit in the most barren of places. Even while nailed to the cross he was still saving sinners, winning for his kingdom one of the thieves crucified beside him. And even in the grave his leaf did not wither, for God raised him in the splendour of the resurrection. Jesus is *the* blessed man. The good news is that he did this all *for us,* living the life we should have lived and dying the death we deserved to die beneath the righteous wrath of God. His blessing overthrows our curse, and bestows life to all who come to God by him.

Let me put this differently. Surely the message of Psalm 1 is that the way to blessing is righteousness. The secret of life is that we should seek after holiness, not happiness. Jesus taught this when he said, 'Seek first his kingdom and his righteousness, and all these things will be given to you as well' (*Matt.* 6:33). But how, then, are sinners like us to be blessed? The answer is through the gospel of the Lord Jesus Christ only by which we receive the forgiveness of sin, righteousness, and the Holy Spirit's power to live a new life to the glory of God. 'God made him who had no sin to be sin for us', Paul writes of Christ, 'so that in him we might become the righteousness of God' (*2 Cor.* 5:21). Therefore the way of blessing for us is in and through Jesus Christ; it is through faith in him and in the power of the Spirit that Christians live out the blessed life portrayed in this psalm.

Jesus said, 'I have come that they may have life, and have it to the full' (*John* 10:10). 'If anyone is thirsty', he says, 'let him come to me and drink. Whoever believes in me . . . streams of living water will flow from within him' (*John* 7:37–38). The Bible ends with a vision of heaven as a city, with 'the river of the water of life, as clear as crystal, flowing from the throne of God and of the Lamb' (*Rev.* 22:1). That is the blessed destiny for those who trust in Christ. Jesus proclaimed, in the last beatitude recorded in God's Word, 'Blessed are those who wash their robes, that they may have the right to the tree of life and may go through the gates into the city' (*Rev.* 22:14). The invitation is open to all: '"Come!" And let him who hears say, "Come!" Whoever is thirsty, let him come; and whoever wishes, let him take the free gift of the water of life' (*Rev.* 22:17).

Blessed is the man, blessed is the woman, who hears, who believes, and who comes to the Saviour, Jesus Christ, and walks with God through faith in him.

2

WHAT IS MAN?
PSALM 8

O LORD, our Lord, how majestic is your name in all the earth! . . .
What is man that you are mindful of him, and the son of man
that you care for him? (*Psa.* 8:1, 4).

I f we are going to walk with God, we need first to have a
proper perspective on ourselves, on the world, and on our
relationship to God. To put this differently, the Bible provides a
whole view of life for us to embrace. Perhaps the best example
is David's hymn of praise to God in Psalm 8. This psalm presents
King David's poetic response to the impression made on his heart
as he gazes on the heavens at night. It begins and ends with
praise for God's majesty and in reply asks, 'What is man?' (verse
4). Derek Kidner describes it as 'an unsurpassed example of what
a hymn should be, celebrating as it does the glory and grace of
God, rehearsing who He is and what He has done, and relating
us and our world to Him; all with a masterly economy of words
and in a spirit of mingled joy and awe'.[1]

[1] Derek Kidner, *Psalms 1–72* (Downers Grove, Ill.: InterVarsity, 1973),
pp. 65–6.

A Biblical Worldview

Everyone has and needs a worldview. According to Brian J. Walsh and J. Richard Middleton, a worldview is a model of reality by which we interpret the world around us. From this come our values, our sense of what is and what is not important, our ideas of how things ought to be, and how we should live.[2]

Walsh and Middleton say that a worldview depends on the answers to four basic questions. First we ask, 'Who am I?' That is, what is the nature, task, and purpose of human beings? Next is, 'Where am I?' Or, what is the nature of the world in which I live? Third is, 'What is wrong?' What is the basic problem that keeps me from attaining fulfilment? Fourth we ask, 'What is the remedy?' How can I overcome this hindrance to my fulfilment . . . how do I find salvation?[3] 'Who am I?', 'Where am I?', 'What is wrong?', and 'What is the remedy?'

Psalm 8 has much to say in answer to these questions. Its key question is 'What is man that you are mindful of him?' (verse 4). This relates to the first worldview issue: 'Who am I?' Verse 5 provides us with the answer, 'You made him.' Man is a creature made by God. Furthermore, we learn here that man is a spiritual being, occupying a mediating position between heaven and earth, since he was made for both. 'You made him a little lower than the heavenly beings', David writes, 'and crowned him with glory and honour.' Verses 6–8 speak of our task: 'You made him ruler over the works of your hands; you put everything under his feet.'

Psalm 8 tells us who we are, and does so in terms of our relationship to God. The psalm tells us, 'We will never understand human beings unless we see them as God's creatures and recognize that they have special responsibilities to their Creator.'[4]

---

[2] Brian J. Walsh and J. Richard Middleton, *The Transforming Vision* (Downers Grove, Ill.: InterVarsity, 1984), pp. 31–2. [3] Ibid., p. 34.
[4] James M. Boice, *Psalms*, 3 vols. (Grand Rapids: Baker, 1994), vol. 1, p. 67.

The second worldview question is: 'Where am I?' The answer of Psalm 8 is that we live in a world created by and for God. The opening verses tell us that the heavens declare his majesty and through his creation he has 'ordained praise'. We live in a purposeful world, one that derives its existence and meaning from God and the pursuit of his glory.

Just these two worldview questions provide us with defining values and beliefs. This is why worldviews are so important. Consider Nihilism, for instance, a worldview very opposed to Christianity. It says we are meaningless creatures in a pointless world that is going nowhere. This worldview bequeaths the values of hopelessness, despair, and cruelty. Or take Existentialism, another non-Christian worldview. It views us as sensual beings living only in the present moment, and it instils the values of a chaotic, self-absorbed hedonism. What, then, are the products of a Christian and biblical view of the world and life in it? What happens to us when we believe that we are made by God and blessed by God in a world he created for the purpose of showing and sharing his glory? Let me suggest three products of the biblical worldview that are clearly evident in the text of this psalm: wonder, humility, and dignity.

The Gift of Wonder

The purpose of our studies in this book is to give us insight into the subject of communion with God. What is it to know God and to walk with him through this life? First, it is to be open to the *wonder* of God's presence. David looks up to the starry sky and exclaims, 'O LORD, our Lord, how majestic is your name in all the earth!'

He is not closed in to the realm of nature only, but perceives the hand of God revealed in the world. 'You have set your glory above the heavens', he exclaims. Perhaps he then hears the cry of a baby in the night, and this too reminds him of the glory of God: 'From the lips of children and infants you have ordained praise' (verse 2). The moon and the stars above, and the baby's cry below, testify to God's handiwork and David, contemplating these things, is filled with wonder and awe. Old Testament scholar E. J. Young puts into words the believer's wonder toward God:

> The entirety of creation, visible and invisible, speaks with voices clear and positive of the glory of the Holy God. Wherever we turn our eyes, we see the marks of His majesty, and should lift our hearts in praise to Him who is holy. This is His world, the wide theatre in which His perfect glory is displayed.[5]

For this reason, I often find myself marvelling at how wonderful it is for us to be Christians, to have our eyes open to such wonder and excitement in all of life. You are at a wedding and instead of seeing just two people making promises and trying to find some happiness, you see God reaching into our world and giving a gift of loving companionship, as in Eden of old.

You hear music and beyond the melody and harmony and movement, you realize that there is an infinite God of order, in whom numberless combinations are held together and made beautiful. The wonder of God's glory shines forth in all our world. How wonderful to see it, to perceive the Creator's hand, and through his hand to know his heart. Charles Spurgeon exclaims:

> When by night we lift up our eyes and behold him who hath created all these things; when we remember that he brings out their host by number, calls them all by their names, and that by the greatness of his power not one falls, then indeed we adore a mighty God, and our soul naturally falls prostrate in reverential awe before the throne of him who leads the host of heaven, and marshals the stars in their armies.[6]

[5] E.J. Young: *Isaiah*, 3 vols. (Grand Rapids: Eerdmans, 1972), vol. 1, pp. 245–6.
[6] C. H. Spurgeon: *Spurgeon's Sermons*, 10 Vols. (Grand Rapids: Baker, 1883), vol. 2, p. 18.

G. Campbell Morgan tells of a meeting he had as a boy with an older man who had been converted to Christ through the ministry of his father. A few days after the man's conversion, Morgan encountered him in a garden. He was holding something small and gazing into his hand with a sense of obvious wonder. Morgan asked him what it was, and with a voice filled with awe the man showed him a leaf that had fallen from a tree. He replied, 'The beauty of God!'

In striking contrast is the experience of Charles Darwin, the father of the theory of evolution. He turned his back on God and committed himself to secular humanism. His biography reveals that in so doing he lost his taste for life. As he grew older, he admitted that he could no longer get anything out of poetry, out of music, out of art. Life lost its flavour for him and he lived out his days in a world without wonder and awe.

David looks up to the sky at night and exclaims, 'O LORD, our Lord, how majestic is your name in all the earth!' What David saw with the eyes of faith, an increasing number of scientists today are forced to admit. I refer to the evidence of design in the world.

Why is our planet just the right size to sustain a liveable atmosphere? Why is the earth just the right distance from the sun so that we neither burn up nor freeze? Why is the moon just the right size and distance from us so that the oceans are neither stagnant nor out of control? The only plausible answer to these and a myriad other similar questions is that it was designed this way for us. The same traces of design are found at every level of exploration – not just in astronomy – but in the very structure of the universe at the greatest macro and the smallest micro levels. All of creation testifies to a Maker; it cries, 'O LORD, our Lord, how majestic is your name!'

David comprehended this great truth without the tools of modern science. The same was true when he heard the baby's cry. Science tells us today what an incredible feat it is that a human cell multiplies until a little baby is held in his mother's arms and cries. The instructions found in the DNA of a newly formed human cell are estimated to contain enough information to fill a thousand 600-page books. We are proud of the little we know about DNA, but what of the God who conceived it! David's ears, apart from our scientific instruction, heard infant wails and knew they praised our Maker. 'From the lips of children and infants you have ordained praise' (verse 2). That is enough, he says, to silence every foe of God – the cry from the lips of infants.

Contend, he says, with the Maker of this child! Set beside this the works of your own hands! Reckon with the power that brought both the galaxies and infants into being! Oh, the wonder of God in all creation! We are the first to admit that this world has gone wrong. Yes, the baby's cry is too often one of hunger or abuse – that, sadly is fallen man's contribution to what God made good at the beginning. We do not have the right to accuse God for the suffering that takes place in this world, but rather it is God who demands an account of this suffering from us. Even when the baby's cry testifies against our sin, there is still the baby itself – the marvel of God's creation that radiates his majestic glory.

That, of course, prompts a question. Do you know anything about what I am saying? Do you walk through the streets and see immortal creatures made by God, or only dull, impersonal faces? Have you ever looked at a leaf and praised God for its intricate design, delicacy, and amazing strength? Or do you live in a dreary grey world, devoid of the holy, with no wonder, no awe, no praise? Have you ever sung with a sincere sense of worship the words of the great hymn:

> Holy, holy, holy, Lord God Almighty!
> All thy works shall praise thy name
> in earth and sky and sea!

Do you know anything of that wonder? If not, turn your heart to God and ask him to reveal himself to your soul. Jesus said,

'Ask, and it will be given to you; seek, and you will find; knock, and it will be opened to you' (*Luke* 11:9).

Humility before God

A Christian worldview, one that sees and knows the presence of God in the world, opens to us the wonder we see in this psalm. Another product of a Christian worldview is *humility*. 'When I look at your heavens, the work of your fingers, the moon and the stars, which you have set in place', David muses, 'what is man that you are mindful of him, and the son of man that you care for him?' (verses 3–4). Instead of the inflated idea of self so prevalent today, the psalmist's awareness of God's majesty and power makes him amazed to think that God cares about us at all. John Stott points out that our knowledge of the universe today, vastly greater than David's, ought to inspire, not a lesser, but a greater sense of humility. He writes:

> If this was David's reaction, nearly 3,000 years ago, how much more should it be ours who live in days of astro-physics and the conquest of space? As we consider the orbiting planets of our solar system, so infinitesimally small in comparison with countless galaxies millions of light-years distant, it may seem to us incredible that the great God of the universe should take any note of us at all, let alone care for us. Yet, he does; and Jesus assured us that even the hairs of our head are all numbered.[7]

Indeed, here is a ready test to determine if someone has really come to know God. All through the Bible we find that when people stand before God they are immediately aware of how small they are as creatures and how unworthy because of sin. This is how the Book of Job concludes. Job, the suffering man, had thrown his questions at God, and the Lord finally answered him out of a great storm (*Job* 38:1). Job saw God in his awful majesty and cried, 'I had heard of you by the hearing of the ear,

---

[7] John Stott, *Favorite Psalms: Growing Closer to God* (Grand Rapids: Baker, 2003), p. 10.

but now my eye sees you; therefore I despise myself, and repent in dust and ashes' (*Job* 42:5). The prophet Isaiah had a similar experience, which he relates in the sixth chapter of his prophecy. He prostrated himself at the sight of God's majesty, crying, 'Woe to me! For I am lost; for I am a man of unclean lips, and I dwell in the midst of a people of unclean lips; for my eyes have seen the King, the LORD of hosts!' (*Isa.* 6:5).

This also happened to Simon Peter the fisherman, after he took a preacher by the name of Jesus into his boat. Peter had been fishing all night and hadn't caught a thing, so Jesus told him to let down his nets at a certain place. 'A typical know-it-all preacher', Peter may have thought. 'Imagine telling a fisherman like me how to fish!' But when the nets were filled to bursting, Peter knew he was in the presence of someone who was much more than a preacher. The Son of God was the passenger in his boat! He fell to his knees, crying, 'Depart from me, for I am a sinful man, O Lord' (*Luke* 5:8).

When we see God, when we are able to say with the psalmist, 'O LORD, our Lord, how majestic is your name in all the earth!', it humbles us by giving us an awareness of our sinfulness. What a marvel that this God should ever have set his affection on creatures like us!

The importance of this is illustrated in the life of Nebuchadnezzar, the all-conquering Babylonian king. At the height of his career, Nebuchadnezzar was filled with a sense of his own glory and might. Looking out over his glorious city, he spoke words that typify the sinful attitude of all mankind in its pride. 'Is not this great Babylon, which I have built by my mighty power as a royal residence and for the glory of my majesty?' (*Dan.* 4:30). James Boice calls this 'a classic statement of what we today call secular humanism, describing creation as of man, by man, and for man's glory'.[8] That is man in his pride, something we know all about today. The next verse tells us how God responded: 'While the words were still in the king's mouth,

[8] Boice, *Psalms*, vol. 1, p. 71.

there fell a voice from heaven, 'O King Nebuchadnezzar, to you it is spoken: The kingdom has departed from you, and you shall be driven from among men, and your dwelling shall be with the beasts of the field. And you shall be made to eat grass like an ox, and seven periods of time shall pass over you, until you know that the Most High rules the kingdom of men and gives it to whom he will' (*Dan.* 4:31–32).

This was not an arbitrary judgment. By cursing him with insanity, God gave his assessment of what the king had said while looking on the world in his pride. God was saying, 'If you believe that, if you look on the wonders of this world and think that a puny human being like yourself is responsible for such greatness, then you must be out of your mind.' God illustrated through Nebuchadnezzar's experience that we only come to our right mind when we acknowledge 'that the Most High rules the kingdom of men' (*Dan.* 4:32), and that every good gift comes from God and is for the praise of his Name.

A Little beneath God

First, we see the joyful *wonder* that comes to those who know God, who look on life with a biblical worldview. Second, this gives us creatures a right *humility* before the awesome God who made us. But, third, we see the *dignity* that comes to men and women as they understand their place in God's economy. We see this in verses 5–8:

> You have made him a little lower than the heavenly beings and crowned him with glory and honour. You have given him dominion over the works of your hands; you have put all things under his feet, all sheep and oxen, and also the beasts of the field, the birds of the heavens, and the fish of the sea, whatever passes along the paths of the seas.

Man's dignity comes from God's creation of him. 'You made him a little lower than the heavenly beings.' The Hebrew text actually says, 'You made him a little lower than God', using

Elohim, the Hebrew word for God. The Septuagint translators of the Old Testament rendered this with the Greek word for angels, partly because there are cases where *Elohim* means 'spirits' or 'angels' (*1 Sam.* 28:13; *Psa.* 82), and perhaps, out of modesty. It is following this precedent that Hebrews 2:7 quotes this verse in speaking about Jesus: 'You made him a little lower than the angels.'

The point is that Psalm 8 grounds man's dignity in that he was created in the image of God. J. A. Alexander translates verse 5 by saying God 'removed him little from divinity'.[9] Man is not God, but we are made with something God-like in our nature. We made this point earlier in asking the question, 'Who are we?' God placed something of himself into us and we bear his image. Genesis 2:7 says God breathed into the first man and he 'became a living creature'. We have minds endowed with reason and understanding and in this we are different from the rest of creation; we are above it, possessing responsibility and power to exercise dominion under God.

If our dignity comes from our relationship to God, no wonder we have so much degradation in our world today. God has been removed and man is now defined in animal terms, just a bit further along the evolutionary scale than the beasts. By denying God we have rejected our true dignity as special mediating beings, God's stewards in his creation.

Notice that the psalm places us between heaven and earth, but it is in terms of heaven that we receive our identity. It does not describe us as 'a little above the beasts', but 'a little lower than God'.

People justify all kinds of depravity today on the basis of how the animals act. The result is a beastly human race. But Psalm 8 tells us that we are to look upward to God and not downward to the animals. We are made by God in his own image to govern God's creation for his pleasure and glory. Our dignity, then, is

9 Joseph A. Alexander, *The Psalms Translated and Explained* (Grand Rapids: Baker, 1977), p. 89.

only realized in our relationship to God, in our calling from God, and ultimately as we live according to God's will in his world.

The World's Problem and Remedy

That, however, presents us with the great problem we face. As we have seen, a worldview is concerned with four questions, the first two of which are 'Who am I?' and 'Where am I?' The Bible says we are men and women made in God's image and placed in the world that was made for God's glory. Understanding these things we gain a sense of wonder, humility, and dignity. Yet now we must confront the third question, 'What is wrong with the world?'

The answer is obvious, that we have forfeited our blessings by turning from God in sin. Paul says of mankind in Romans 1:21, 25: 'Although they knew God, they did not honour him as God or give thanks to him . . . they exchanged the truth about God for a lie and worshipped and served the creature rather than the Creator.' Instead of looking up to God to give him glory, man has looked down to the earth to take glory for himself. That is the essence of sin and from it flow all the great problems of the world.

I mentioned earlier that the second chapter of Hebrews picks up on this psalm. It notes that we do not actually experience the reality of what Psalm 8 says: 'You crowned him with glory and honour. You made him ruler over the works of your hands; you put everything under his feet.' But that is not what we see now, is it?

The evidence before us is not that of God's image borne by obedient mankind but an image shattered by disobedience and sin. Ours is not the story of dominion embraced and cultivated under God, but paradise lost in rebellion. If God has placed everything under man's feet, then something has gone wrong badly, for if we list those things very obviously not under man's control the list quickly becomes quite large. Man is largely at the mercy of the weather; our food supply, even today, is greatly influenced by forces outside the farmer's control. Mankind is starving, bleeding, crying, and suffering all over this globe. Hurricanes and droughts, tornadoes and floods, these beat against man with unmastered fury. Indeed, man is not able to control his own self, his own passions, even his own thoughts. A quick look at the newspaper will display this as we read about international as well as individual crises all over the world. Hebrews 2:8 sums this up, in response to Psalm 8, 'At present, we do not yet see everything in subjection to him.'

That is the problem, and according to the Bible it is all the result of sin ultimately – our first parents' sin and our own sin. We have looked away from God and become like beasts; through our disobedience we no longer reflect his image in the world, we have sinfully rebelled against our Maker.

That is the problem. However, the writer of Hebrews sees the answer in this psalm as well. Sinful man has fallen from dominion into the bondage of sin and the futility of death. But there is a remedy. There is another man to whom these words apply, a mediator who has not forfeited his glory or dominion. Hebrews 2:8–9 presents the problem and the answer: 'In putting everything in subjection to him, God left nothing that is outside his control. At present, we do not yet see everything in subjection to him. But we see him who for a little while was made lower than the angels, namely Jesus, crowned with glory and honour because of the suffering of death, so that by the grace of God he might taste death for everyone.' Sin is the problem, and Jesus is the answer. He came into our human condition and was faithful to God. By his sacrificial death he redeemed us from our sin so that we can enter with him into the reclaimed dignity of his resurrection life as the children of God.

At the heart of Psalm 8 is the question, 'What is man?' If we look around this world we have to answer that man is a fallen being, one who has rebelled against his God-given identity and task, and who has lost his original station and dignity. But the

Bible does not leave us with that sad and tragic fact. Instead it points us to the new man, the Second Adam, the Lord Jesus Christ.

Behold the Man!

This could not have been expressed more eloquently than it was by Pontius Pilate, at a crucial moment in the life of Jesus. The Jews had brought Jesus before the Roman governor, falsely accusing him of blasphemy and insurrection. Pilate's investigation found no evidence of wrongdoing. Pilate himself declared the righteousness of Jesus: 'I find no guilt in him' (*John* 18:38). Nonetheless, acting on behalf of man in rebellion against God, Pilate had Jesus beaten, mocked, and brutally scourged by whips. Blood streaming down Jesus' battered face, a crown of thorns pressed into his brow, Pilate brought forth our Lord before the crowds. Psalm 8 asks, 'What is man?' and Pilate gave the epic answer, declaring of Jesus, 'Behold the man!' (*John* 19:5).

Oh, the eloquence of God! It is not the dignity of worldly acclaim, nor the glory of fleshly pomp, nor the beauty of rich jewels and a fine appearance that makes a man what he ought to be. It is the obedience shown by Jesus Christ, the obedience of his life, and especially his death on the cross, that pleases God. Jesus regained by righteousness what mankind had lost by sin. It is in union with Christ through faith that men and women are cleansed from their sins and restored to God: restored to the wonder of knowing God, to the humility that comes from seeing God, to the dignity that arises from God's transforming work as he enables us once more, in Christ, to do his will.

Pilate set forth Jesus, saying, 'Behold the man!' The crowd rejected him and sent him off to death on a cross. People still reject Jesus today, choosing the deadly rule of sin, the false dignity of rebellion against their Maker. But that is not the last word. God raised Jesus from the grave, thus declaring him the true man acceptable to God and exalting him to all authority in heaven and earth. Some day soon that same Jesus will return in glory and might, with the company of God's holy angels. Philippians 2:10–11 says this was so that, 'at the name of Jesus every knee should bow, in heaven and on earth and under the earth, and every tongue confess that Jesus Christ is Lord, to the glory of God the Father.' Every sinner will then admit, 'Yes, that is what I should have been.' Every tongue that rejected him as Saviour will declare him Lord over all to their own eternal disgrace.

But what of you? What if you behold the man Jesus Christ, God's own Son, and see that, because of your sin, you are not the man or woman you were meant to be, realizing the offence you have given to God, and the judgment you have earned? What if you ask Jesus to cleanse you with his blood and to clothe you in his perfect righteousness? Then one day an angel will look on you and ask the question, 'What is this man? Is this not one of that race made just a little below God but which fell into disgrace and destruction because of sin?' And another angel will answer, 'Yes, but he is one of those for whom God sent his own Son to die and rise again. He has been washed in the blood of the Lamb, and in Jesus Christ has regained all that was lost and more. He has been crowned with a glory and honour that will never fade and we are now ministering servants to him.'

In that age to come, the Bible says, all who have trusted in Christ will shine like the stars in the heavens (*Dan.* 12:3). And gazing on us, the angels themselves will turn to God and sing the words of praise that complete this psalm: 'O LORD, our Lord, how majestic is your name in all the earth!'

3

My Lord, My Shepherd
Psalm 23

The LORD is my shepherd; I shall not want. He makes me lie down in green pastures. He leads me beside still waters. He restores my soul. He leads me in paths of righteousness for his name's sake (*Psa.* 23:1–3).

'The LORD is my shepherd.' There are few phrases more familiar and more comforting to those who know and love the Bible. Psalm 23 is often one of the first passages that wins a permanent place in the believer's heart. It is among the first we teach our children; it is not hard to imagine our Lord Jesus learning to repeat these words in Hebrew as a little child. It is among the last words heard by many departing from this life in death. My own father breathed his last while I read the words of Psalm 23 into his ear. Its powerful influence over our hearts stems from its message that a caring God will meet our deepest needs. It puts into precious words the relationship a Christian has with the Lord.

We talk about having a personal relationship with God. But for many that is an elusive concept. God is not like other people, with whom we talk in face-to-face communication. If God is present, he is not seen; if he speaks, he does not do so audibly; if he is with me, I am not always sure of it. How, then, do I relate to God? Psalm 23 answers these questions by giving us a depiction of a sheep's trust in its shepherd. These verses take us by the hand and give us reasons to trust God in every circumstance of life, just as the sheep wholly relies on its shepherd. Psalm 23, says one writer, 'breathes throughout a spirit of the calmest and most assured trust in God: it speaks of a peace so deep, a serenity so profound, that even the thought of the shadow of death cannot trouble it'.[1]

Shepherd and Sheep

The psalm begins with its defining statement, 'The LORD is my shepherd.' The word LORD is in the Hebrew *Yahweh* or *Jehovah*, the personal covenant name of God. It speaks of God's self-existent sufficiency. The name's meaning was told to Moses at the burning bush: 'I AM WHO I AM' (*Exod.* 3:14). This is the eternal God, who has life in himself, and who unchangeably remains the same. It is *this* God, *Yahweh*, whom David calls 'my shepherd'.

We may not realize what an astonishing statement this is. In Israel, as in other ancient societies, a shepherd was looked down upon as a lower-class worker. It was the youngest son, like David, who took on this unpleasant assignment. Shepherding was onerous, requiring twenty-four-hour-a-day involvement. And yet God, who calls himself the 'helper of Israel', has taken upon himself this humble service. In so doing, he commends the same humility and spirit of self-sacrificing ministry to us.

The fact that God is our shepherd also describes the tenderness of his personal involvement for our care. Phillip Keller, who was himself a shepherd in East Africa for many years, where much of the ancient practice of shepherding continues, has written a beautiful book titled *A Shepherd Looks at Psalm 23*. In it he

[1] J. J. Stewart Perowne, *The Book of Psalms* (Grand Rapids: Zondervan, 1976), p. 248.

shares insights into this psalm from his own extensive experience:

> The welfare of any flock is entirely dependent upon the management afforded them by their owner . . . For Him there is no greater reward, no deeper satisfaction, than that of seeing His sheep well contented, well fed, safe and flourishing under His care . . . He will go to no end of trouble and labour to supply them with the finest grazing, the richest pasturage, ample winter feed, and clean water . . . From early dawn until late at night this utterly selfless Shepherd is alert to the welfare of His flock.[2]

That is an uplifting statement, but it calls us to an understanding of ourselves that may not be so uplifting. If God is our shepherd, then biblically speaking, we are likened to sheep! This is not a flattering comparison. Sheep are helpless and stupid. They are easily panicked, annoyed, and debilitated. 'Unable to defend themselves against wolves, they also need protecting from themselves; sheep are notorious for wandering off good pastures or away from sources of water, for destroying what good grass is available, and for placing themselves in one irretrievable situation after another.'[3] That is, in fact, what we are like spiritually. Charles Spurgeon shares this insight:

> There is no animal (except a man), that has so many forms of sickness as a sheep has. It may be afflicted in any part of its body, from its feet up to its head . . . Sheep have a great number of follies. If there is a hole in the hedge, they are sure to find it out, and press through . . . They are prone to wander, and ready for all sorts of mischief, but they never assist the shepherd in the slightest degree. In this respect, we are all just like the silly sheep, yet, our good Shepherd supplies all the needs, pities all the infirmities, and pardons all the wanderings of his poor wayward flock.[4]

[2] Phillip Keller, *A Shepherd Looks at Psalm 23* (Chicago: Moody, 1970), pp. 21–4.
[3] Richard D. Phillips, *The Heart of an Executive: Lessons on Leadership from the Life of King David* (New York: Doubleday, 1999), p. 6.
[4] C. H. Spurgeon, *Metropolitan Tabernacle Pulpit*, vol. 52, pp. 462–3.

There is one positive thing we can say about sheep, and that is they always have a shepherd. Spurgeon comments, 'A sheep is an object of property, not a wild animal; its owner sets great store by it, and frequently it is bought with a great price.'[5] That is why we are so comforted by this psalm. It evokes a feeling of security, and reassures us that God is interested, involved, and in control of our lives. The main thought pulsing through this most lovely of psalms is that of trust in God. That is why David rejoices in his heart and presents to us these matchless verses of praise and confidence in his God. Because the Lord is our shepherd, David informs the weak, struggling, threatened Christian of three things: we shall not *want*, we need not *fear*, and we will not *fail*.

I Shall Not Want

Sheep are always on the move. Not only does the shepherd rotate his flock among his pastures, but the sheep make an annual pilgrimage from the low winter grazing lands up to the high pastures for the summer. I think that movement, which would have been so familiar to David, is reflected in this psalm. Comparing himself to a sheep and looking ahead to his own trek through life, he says, 'The LORD is my shepherd, I shall not want.' J. J. Stewart Perowne writes, 'As [David] had watched over, and provided for, and tended his flock, leading them to the greenest pastures, and finding for them the water which in that country was so scarce, and guarding them by night from beasts of prey, so he felt his God would provide for and watch over him.'[6]

Many of us can think of things we lack in life. But as God is the shepherd of our souls we find that every spiritual thing we need is in fact provided by him, whether we are rich or poor in material possessions. Verses 2–3 speak of three ways in which God provides for us: *rest*, *restoration*, and *guidance*.

[5] C. H. Spurgeon, *Treasury of David*, 3 vols. (Peabody: Hendrickson, n.d.), vol. 1, pp. 353–4.   [6] Perowne, p. 250.

Verse 2 says, 'He makes me lie down in green pastures. He leads me beside still waters.' The Bible promises food for the souls of God's hungry people; their spiritual thirst will be satisfied, and should they grow weary, Christ will give them rest. 'I am the bread of life', Jesus said. 'Whoever comes to me shall not hunger, and whoever believes in me shall never thirst' (*John* 6:35). 'Come to me, all who labour and are heavy laden, and I will give you rest' (*Matt.* 11:28). This is what David captures in this lovely verse. Perowne says of it, 'Certainly no image could have been devised more beautifully descriptive of rest and safety and trustful happiness, than that of the sheep lying down in the deep, rich meadow-grass, beside the living stream, under the care of a tender and watchful shepherd.'[7] With the peace he gives, God is able to make his sheep lie down comfortably in any circumstance; under his loving care any pasture can be made green and lush for the soul.

To this scene of rest and refreshment verse 3 adds, 'He restores my soul.' This is the second provision about which David speaks. God restores us in a variety of ways depending on our situation. He may rest us and feed us when our souls are faint. In David's case, God restored him by sending the prophet Nathan to rebuke him for his great sin with Bathsheba. God is able to restore every sheep that falters or falls, gently or sternly according to our need.

The word for *soul* may also be rendered as *life*, so that the meaning may be that our divine Shepherd rescues our life. Keller points out a common problem known to shepherds as 'cast (or cast down) sheep'. A sheep will sometimes lie down and roll over, shifting its centre of gravity so that it turns all the way over on its back. When that happens the animal panics and thrashes violently. Stomach gases build up and cut off circulation from the legs so that the sheep may die within a few hours. It is only the shepherd who can restore the sheep, turning it over and saving its life. How often we are just like that. Spiritually

[7] Ibid., p. 248.

we are on our backs, helpless as cast sheep. But the Lord comes to us. He rights us, restores our lives, and returns us to the fold.

The third provision spoken of in verses 2–3 is guidance: 'He leads me in paths of righteousness for his name's sake.' Keller states that sheep typically follow the crowd along the well-worn path, which quickly turns into a worthless rut. The same is true of us, blindly following the ways of the world. But the shepherd leads the sheep on to a different path. David calls it the righteous path, which is wholesome and brings credit to our shepherd. This is what Christians find as they trust and obey God's Word. It is the path of righteousness that leads to lush fields, whereas the ruts where the untended sheep go are ruined and leave them impoverished and weak.

'The LORD is my shepherd', David exults, 'I shall not want.' His attitude is one of contentment and joy. The result of this attitude is a confidence in God that enables the Christian to withstand the temptations and allurements of the world.

An episode from the life of Abraham illustrates the importance of such confidence in God. In Genesis 13 we find that God enlarged the flocks of Abram and his nephew Lot to such an extent that they needed to go their separate ways into different lands. Content with God's provision, Abram sacrificed his right as the older man of first choice, and gave Lot his pick of the land. 'If you take the left hand', he said, 'then I will go to the right, or if you take the right hand, then I will go to the left' (*Gen.* 13:9). The Bible says that Lot looked down on the fertile region of the Jordan River and chose to dwell there, despite its proximity to the most sinful cities in the land, Sodom and Gomorrah. Genesis 13:12 says, 'Lot settled among the cities of the valley and moved his tent as far as Sodom.' The result of that choice would become significant, for Sodom exerted a stronger influence on Lot than Lot did on Sodom. Before long Lot was living in the wicked city and was enmeshed in its sinful affairs. His story is a sad one, for when God judged Sodom,

Lot lost all that he had, and his wife and daughters were converted to the sinful ways of that city. Like so many foolish Christians who lack confidence in God, he thought he had to live close to the world to get on in life, despite the obvious compromise with sin.

Abram, however, kept far from the cities of sin and dwelt in the apparently less fertile lands of Canaan, counting on the Lord to keep him from want. God rewarded his faith with a great promise of blessing. He said, 'Lift up your eyes from where you are and look north and south, east and west. All the land that you see I will give to you and your offspring for ever' (*Gen.* 13:14). Many of us, no doubt, need to lift up our eyes from the glittering baubles of the world to the promises of the living God. 'The LORD is my shepherd; I shall not want', says the Psalmist. If we can say that, we will then follow him in the paths of righteousness, with peace and joy in our hearts and seeking above everything else to bring glory to his Name.

I Shall Not Fear

The second blessing from having the Lord as our shepherd is expressed in verse 4, perhaps the most well-known line in this most famous of psalms: 'Even though I walk through the valley of the shadow of death, I will fear no evil, for you are with me; your rod and your staff, they comfort me.' David knows there is evil and danger (just as we should), but because his Shepherd is with him he will not fear.

Keller vividly pictures this in terms of the flock's seasonal passage from the lowlands, where the sheep feed in winter, to the high pastures in summer, passing through the valleys on the way. These valleys are rich and fertile but they are also dangerous. Wild animals lurk in the canyons and shadows; flash floods sweep through with little notice.

It is important to realize that the path of righteousness does lead us through dark valleys. Trials must not be interpreted as signs that we are 'out of God's will'. Rather, God takes us through trials and dangers to develop our character and faith and to lead us to spiritual maturity. David explicitly calls this 'the valley of the shadow of death'. It may be, therefore, that David is thinking especially of our greatest trial, our passage through death into the life to come. We do fear danger, especially death. But David says even of this, 'I will fear no evil, for you are with me.'

Let us observe the fact that David sees us passing *through* the valley. It is not our final destination, but only a passage we must make, and one which leads to greener, safer fields beyond. This is true of every trial, but most eminently of a Christian's death. Second, the valley through which we must pass holds only *the shadow* of death. Death is but a shadow across the path of believers. Matthew Henry comments, 'There is no substantial evil in it; the shadow of a serpent will not sting nor the shadow of a sword kill.'[8] Likewise, Christ having removed the sting from death, all that remains for us is death's shadow, which cannot harm us. Death is like a cloud that passes by and blocks the sun from the eyes for a while. But the eye of faith knows there is a light behind the shadow, and waits without fear for the shadow's passing. So it is with every trial, every shadow, and especially death. We will pass through to safety, ultimately reaching lush pastures in the higher lands where the sun shines brightly.

But what most greatly relieves the heart from fear is the presence of the shepherd himself in the midst of the shadow: 'I will fear no evil, for you are with me.' The thoughtful shepherd knows that in danger or difficulty he must be visible to the sheep. Likewise, the Spirit of the Lord comes near to the fearful Christian who trusts in God's Word. I think one of the Bible's most precious promises is found in Isaiah 43. God says, 'When you pass through the waters, I will be with you; and through the rivers, they shall not overwhelm you; when you walk through fire you shall not be burned, and the flame shall not

---

[8] Matthew Henry, *Commentary on the Whole Bible*, 6 vols. (Peabody: Hendrickson, 1992), vol. 3, p. 259.

consume you. For I am the LORD your God, the Holy One of Israel, your Saviour' (*Isa.* 43:2–3). In danger or in fear, especially in the shadow of death itself, Christians find solace in God's Word and in prayer, learning anew that he is with them.

The signs of God's authority and might especially bring comfort to David: 'Your rod and your staff, they comfort me.' The staff is the symbol of the shepherd's authority; with it he keeps order in the flock, taking hold of the neck of the wayward sheep. The rod is his weapon. With it he beats off the wolf and smashes the head of the snake; he also wields it to get the attention of unruly sheep. Christians likewise draw comfort from the knowledge that God rules over his flock and protects it with all-powerful might. Knowing his presence and care, Christians can say of every shadow: 'I will not fear it.'

I Shall Not Fail

In the last two verses, many commentators believe the psalm moves from the imagery of a shepherd leading his flock to a host serving a banquet to his guests: 'You prepare a table before me in the presence of my enemies; you anoint my head with oil; my cup overflows.' But in my view, this line of interpretation is not warranted. David has been talking about himself as a man all along, using the familiar metaphor of a sheep and its shepherd. Now, as the psalm climaxes, the boundary between the two simply fades. In these final verses we see the flock's annual pilgrimage coming to its end; this is fully connected to all that has gone before it.

Keller's insights as a shepherd are again helpful. He views verse 5 as speaking of the high table-lands or *mesas* to which the sheep are led for cool summer pasturing. The shepherd prepares these tables in advance of the flock, removing physical hazards, destroying poisonous plants and driving predators away. When David adds the statement of verse 6, 'I shall dwell in the house of the LORD for ever', the Christian cannot fail to think of the heavenly home Jesus has gone ahead to prepare for us. He said,

'In my Father's house are many rooms; if it were not so, would I have told you that I go to prepare a place for you?' (*John* 14:2).

What this tells us, and this is our third major point, is that because the Lord is our shepherd *we will not fail*. Every true Christian will arrive safely in heaven, the place of final, full, and uninterrupted blessing. 'You prepare a table before me in the presence of my enemies' (verse 5). Here, the sheep's table-lands and the wedding banquet of heaven blend together. It is a picture of ultimate acceptance and joyful feasting. There on the high plains the wolves and lions gaze on in frustration, unable to break through to reach the flock. Likewise we shall be safe from every enemy that has sought us in this life – the world, the flesh, and the devil. Before those banished and embittered eyes we shall eat fruit from the tree of life and drink waters from the river of life.

David adds, 'You anoint my head with oil; my cup overflows.' This too brings together blessings enjoyed by sheep and humans alike. Keller recalls the 'joy' with which sheep lift their heads to receive the oil mixed by the shepherd, which soothes and protects their skin and promotes the healing of wounds and diseases. Likewise, ancient hosts provided wine and oil to the weary traveller; oil to soothe the skin and wine to cleanse the dusty throat and gladden the heart. For this reason, a shining face was known as the face of a friend. In Psalm 104:15 David thanks God for 'wine that gladdens the heart of man, oil to make his face shine'.

Here we have a vision of our journey's end, a bright hope that sustains us on our way. Because the Lord is our Shepherd, we will not fail. This is not because we have been strong and worthy, nor because of our works or devotion. The reason we shall not fail is that we are tended and led and protected by the Lord himself. What we really need to pass through the valleys of this life and arrive safely in the eternal bliss of heaven is nothing more and nothing less than to have the Lord as our Shepherd. I want to say this especially to those who are weak and faltering, whose hopes are easily dashed, and whose faith is prone to grow weary. If you will only follow the Lord you will end up safely at your destination – weak, wandering, vulnerable, and sometimes foolish sheep that you are. Why? Because your shepherd is *Yahweh*, the faithful, unchangeable, covenant-keeping God. And along the way you will be fed and strengthened and made to walk in paths of righteousness for his Name's sake.

When we realize how sufficient our Lord is as our Shepherd and Saviour our hearts are filled with peace and joy. 'The LORD is my shepherd', David exults. Therefore he concludes, 'Surely goodness and mercy shall follow me all the days of my life, and I shall dwell in the house of the LORD for ever.' Surely, with that being said, with that sure destination in view, the Christian is ready to follow, strengthened against every fear.

The Good Shepherd

That demands a great question – indeed the great question of life. Is David's Lord your Shepherd? Can you take to yourself the words of this psalm, 'The LORD is *my* shepherd. *I* shall not want. He makes *me* to lie down in green pastures, he leads *me* beside still waters; he restores *my* soul . . . Even though *I* walk through the valley of the shadow of death, *I* will fear no evil, for you are with *me* . . . Surely goodness and mercy will follow *me* all the days of *my* life, and *I* shall dwell in the house of the LORD for ever'?

Many years after it was written, Jesus Christ took this psalm and applied it to himself. He taught that it is only through him that we know God as our shepherd. 'I am the good shepherd', he said (*John* 10:11). 'The sheep hear [the shepherd's] voice. He calls his own sheep by name and leads them out' (*John* 10:3). 'I know my own and my own know me . . . I lay down my life for the sheep' (*John* 10:14–15).

It is Jesus who shepherds God's flock; he is the Lord spoken of here by King David. And it is by coming to him in faith that we become part of his flock. The Lord Jesus cares for us in all the ways we have seen the shepherd caring for his flock – with such energy, diligence and skill. But it is especially by dying on the cross in our place that Jesus demonstrated his marvellous care for his flock. He said, 'I lay down my life for the sheep . . . No one takes it from me, but I lay it down of my own accord' (*John* 10:15,18). Indeed, this is what made us his sheep. Jesus is not a hired servant or herdsman but the owner of the flock – for he purchased us with the coin of his own precious blood. It is through faith in him who shed his blood for the forgiveness of our sins that we are identified as his flock; faith in him as our Saviour brings us the benefits of his saving, shepherding work.

A shepherd like that, who was willing to pay so great a price to take us to himself, will not run away when he sees the wolf threatening. We need to remember that in our trials. Jesus will not shrink from the difficult task of preparing green pastures for us. He will take care to provide us with rest and refreshment, to restore us when we fall on our backs, to lead us in the good and righteous way. Knowing this will supply us with the energy to follow the Lord wherever he chooses to lead. The shepherd who purchased us with his own life's blood will be with us through the valley of the shadow of death so that we need not fear any evil. He will not withhold the staff, and will not spare the rod for either our protection or for our good discipline. He purchased us that we might dwell with him on high, and with him leading the way we will surely arrive there safely, and enjoy the fullness of his love forever. If you know these truths, they will give you faith to follow, and a hope that sheds its light on your darkest path.

Is Jesus your shepherd? If not, then what could possibly keep you from coming to receive his loving care and provision? Do your sins prevent you from coming to him? Surely you can see that the well-worn path of sin never leads to soul-satisfying green pastures and quiet waters. Jesus died to break sin's bondage;

his cross is the gate to the sheep-fold. Draw near to his cross and confess your sins there, and experience, as millions of others have done, the burden of guilt drop from your back. By faith enter into the fold of Jesus the Good Shepherd.

If you have done that, if you can say, 'Yes, the Lord is indeed my shepherd', then surely you ought to stir up your faith in him, renew your love for him and with fresh vigour follow him in the paths of righteousness, where he always leads. 'The LORD is my shepherd.' And if such words are true of you, then so are these: 'Surely goodness and mercy shall follow me all the days of my life, and I shall dwell in the house of the LORD for ever.'

4

I LIFT UP MY EYES
PSALM 121

I lift up my eyes to the hills. From where does my help come? My help comes from the LORD, who made heaven and earth (*Psa.* 121:1–2).

'I lift up my eyes to the hills. From where does my help come? My help comes from the LORD, who made heaven and earth.' There are not many more powerful opening lines in the Psalms than this; here is a memorable expression of need finding its only true provision in God.

Psalm 121 is especially dear to those who face trouble and danger. Together with the twenty-third, it is one of the psalms most dear to many members of the Armed Forces. It is often heard at military funerals, and has become a kind of spiritual credo for both the living and the dead.

Some years ago I served on the faculty of the United States Military Academy at West Point. I remember marching out with the cadets on their way to training, trekking through the mountain terrain along the Hudson River. The chaplain at that time used to post himself on top of a certain promontory, and as each cadet company wearily trudged by, he would cry out from this psalm: 'I lift my eyes to the hills. From where does my help come? My help comes from the LORD.'

I was not surprised, therefore, to read years later of a young commander whose company was ambushed high on a mountain in Afghanistan. After the fight the young officer ministered to his wounded soldiers, urging them to hold on until help could come. He later reported how moved he had been back at West Point by the words of the chaplain on those training exercises. On top of that bleak mountain thousands of miles away, he remembered and softly recited the words of Psalm 121 to his men, one of whom bled to death in his arms. 'I lift up my eyes to the hills', he told them; 'From where does my help come? My help comes from the LORD, who made heaven and earth.'

It has been rightly said that man's extremity is God's opportunity; it is when our earthly hopes fail that our hearts remember to look to the Lord. The Psalmist first looks to the hills, which represent worldly sources of hope. John Calvin explains, 'By the mountains, the [Psalmist] means whatever is great or excellent in the world.'[1] But when hope from there fails, the Psalmist asks a question that has only one true answer: 'From where does my help come?' The only help sufficient to our needs is 'from the LORD'.

Soldiers think of the high ground as a place of security and strength, and by training they look to the hills for help. But when help from there fails they must look elsewhere for protection and aid. The same is true for others in need. Those who are desperately ill look up at the towering medical centre. But after the operation, when the medicines have been taken, and when the hope inspired by doctors and technology has been exhausted, it is to the Lord they must turn. In our economic uncertainty we gaze up to the city skyscrapers but must remind ourselves that our future cannot be secured from the business institutions that have their head offices there. In the midst of

[1] John Calvin, *Commentary on the Book of Psalms*, 6 vols. (Grand Rapids: Baker, 1999) vol. 5, pp. 63–4.

our great international crises we look to the high places of government and power. But is this where our hopes lie? We lift our eyes to all these hills, and we fear, rightly, that they will fail us. Where, then, is our help? In fear, in doubt, in trouble, in pain, we come to the comforting realization that God alone is the One in whom we can and must always depend. Psalm 121 brings before us the truth that when all other help fails, as happens so often, God is a sure and faithful help to those who trust in him.

The Pilgrim's Psalm

Psalm 121 is a 'Psalm of Ascents', as the superscription informs us. That means it probably was one of the psalms sung by the Jews as they made their climb up to the holy city for the religious feasts. One theory holds that it would have been sung at the last encampment on the road to Jerusalem. The weary travellers, seeing Mount Zion and the surrounding hills, sang this psalm to strengthen their tired and aching limbs for the last stage of their journey. Another theory speculates that this psalm was composed for the exiles in Babylon; the hills of Judah were far off and unseen, but, with the eyes of faith, the Lord's exiled people fix their gaze upon God and put their hope in him. Yet another view holds that the hills are the high places where, according to the Old Testament, the idolatrous gods were worshipped. The hills, in this case, were pagan religions which must be rejected so that Yahweh, the one true God, may be trusted.

One thing is sure, multitudes of Christians have turned their thoughts to Psalm 121 in times of uncertainty, especially when embarking on a difficult journey. David Livingstone, the great missionary explorer of Africa, met with his father and sister as he prepared to set out on his dangerous journey. Together they read Psalm 121 and prayed for God's protection. James Montgomery Boice, in his commentary on this psalm, tells of going off to a Christian boarding school while still a young boy.

Years later, he described the powerful impact made upon him by his mother reading this psalm to the whole family, gathered together before he had to leave for school each semester. Time and again she prayed for the kind of protection spoken of here. It was in that way, Boice recalled, that he learned 'the faith of a trusting pilgrim'.[2] Countless other Christians have had similar experiences; Psalm 121 is a comfort to all who walk with God in uncertainty or danger.

The reason this psalm is so dear to pilgrims, to those who journey into darkness or danger, is its insistence on the certainty of God's protection. Its key word is the Hebrew *shamar*, which in its verb or noun form occurs six times in verses 3–8. The English Standard Version helpfully translates this the same way each time, using the English word *keep*. Other versions, such as the New International Version, use both *keep* and *watch*. The idea is of God as our guardian or protector. People like to think of having a guardian angel; it makes them feel safe to know that someone is watching over them. The Bible does speak of guardian angels. But Psalm 121 directs the believer to something even greater, a guardian God who watches over, who keeps, who protects each of his own as they travel through this uncertain world.

Perhaps no story in the Bible demonstrates this more clearly than that of Jacob, who became the father of the nation Israel. Jacob wronged his brother Esau and had to flee for safety. Departing alone into the wilderness, he had no other pillow for his head but a stone, no bed but the cold earth. He was a lonely, fearful traveller. But God came to him and said, 'Behold, I am with you and will keep you wherever you go . . . I will not leave you until I have done what I have promised you' (*Gen.* 28:15). Likewise, Christians may be certain of God's guardian care until his promises of a complete salvation are fully accomplished in our lives.

[2] James Montgomery Boice, *Psalms*, 3 vols. (Grand Rapids: Baker, 1998), vol. 3, p. 1075.

Maker of Heaven and Earth

The Psalmist, in verse 2, reminds us that while every sort of worldly aid is limited and uncertain, God is the great Creator of everything, the one who is infinite in power and might. This is why the Psalmist can find unfailing help in 'the LORD, who made heaven and earth'.

The psalmist is making a contrast between the creation and the Creator. On the one hand we see the hills and all they represent. It is important to note that this psalm does not teach that Christians should shun every kind of earthly help. Christians should go to doctors and take their medicines. We should invest prudently for retirement. We should pray for godly leaders in government. But we must remember that all of these are merely created things and contrast them to the power and strength of the Creator. Every high mountain, every tower, every pinnacle of earthly achievement is a finite, limited thing. However powerful, there is a limit to its might or availability. But none of this can be said of the God of the Bible, who is the Maker of all things. Therefore, when we find our eyes scanning the hills, we should lift them higher still to a greater and more glorious source of help, one more sure, on which we may completely depend.

This reference to God as Creator not only provides a contrast with all creation, but also points to the ease with which God is able to help us in all times of need. God created by his mere Word. God himself is not part of the creation; he does not share its limitations in any way. He is in all places at all times. God sees and knows all things simultaneously. The children's catechism helpfully teaches, 'I cannot see God, but he always sees me.' God can give his full attention to a needy saint on one corner of the globe without being at all distracted from the danger or trouble confronting you. The wisdom with which he considers your plight is the very same wisdom that formed molecules and assembled stars. Almighty power is at his command. Therefore, the help that comes from the Lord, the

Maker of heaven and earth, is all you could ever need, and more. In all of this, God is exalted as the only true God, and this is the reason he demands the exclusive worship of our hearts.

Therefore, the Christian is wise to become acquainted with God, because he is the source of our help and our hope. By knowing him we can experience peace in troubles, and be filled with joy in the midst of trials. Charles Spurgeon remarked: 'The purposes of God; the divine attributes; the providence, predestination, and proved faithfulness of the Lord – these are the hills to which we must lift our eyes, for from these our help must come.' Spurgeon concludes:

> Jehovah who created all things is equal to every emergency; heaven and earth are at the disposal of him who made them, therefore let us be very joyful in our infinite Helper. He will sooner destroy heaven and earth than permit his people to be destroyed, and the perpetual hills themselves shall bow rather than he shall fail whose ways are everlasting. We are bound to look beyond heaven and earth to him who made them both: it is vain to trust the creatures: it is wise to trust the Creator.[3]

A Vigilant Protector

Having reminded us that God is the Creator, the psalm goes on to speak of his vigilance in protecting his people. The last three stanzas, in verses 3 to 8, are organized in stair-step fashion; an idea from one stanza recurs as the building block for the next. This is what truly makes this psalm a song of ascent – an ascent into the security of God's care. What great assurance is given to the believer here! Being persuaded by the truth of these precious words will help us to trust the Lord and have hope in our trials.

First, verse 3 says, 'He will not let your foot be moved.' Imagine a Judean pilgrim wending his way to Jerusalem. How easily his foot might slip on those primitive roads and rock strewn roads! We can extend this idea to misfortune of every

[3] C. H. Spurgeon, *A Treasury of David*, 3 vols. (Peabody: Hendrickson, n.d.), vol. 3, II, pp. 14–15

kind – to sudden changes that threaten to cast us down and hinder our progress. But God is there to steady his people. This is true with regard to temptation and the besetting sins with which we are all so familiar. The one who looks to God will find a steady support that will keep him from falling. Psalm 37:23–24 says, 'The steps of a man are established by the LORD, when he delights in his way; though he fall, he shall not be cast headlong, for the LORD upholds his hand.'

But, alas, Christians often fall, you may say. Increasingly today we hear of believers, often prominent ones, falling into sexual sin or into greed or some other temptation. The reason for such a fall may be that these Christians, regardless of their rank and position, were not walking closely with God. They may have set their eyes on the hills: on power, on pleasure, on worldly success, on their own strength and ability. These cannot keep us from falling. God calls us to walk with him, to draw near to him through prayer, and to obey his Word with sincerity. Only as we walk in his way can we be sure, 'He will not let your foot be moved.'

What if you have strayed from him or have fallen? Then let this verse encourage you to turn back to God. Have you fallen into some sin? Has your foot slipped? Turn to God, confess your sin and ask for his forgiveness and help. He will establish you once again; he will restore your foot on the path, and lead you on the right way.

This stanza offers another angle on God's protection of the pilgrim: 'He who keeps you will not slumber. Behold, he who keeps Israel will neither slumber nor sleep' (verses 3–4). The picture is that of a caravan that has made camp along the way. As darkness falls sentries are posted, but they only do their job effectively if they remain awake and ready. If they fall asleep they will put their people in danger. Our guardian God neither slumbers nor sleeps when darkness gathers round us.

Christians often enter into periods of darkness, times when we cannot see far ahead and where threatening voices intimidate us all around. There are times when we are vulnerable, like sleeping travellers. In such times, we are assured that God is still with us, though the darkness may hide him, though our own weariness causes our eyes to close. Whatever the circumstances into which God has led us, we may rest ourselves peacefully under his care.

The Bible abounds with examples of this. Think of Esther, who lived in a time of great darkness. In exile for their sin, God's people could not see what lay ahead but had to rely on God's unseen providence. God is not mentioned a single time in the Book of Esther; he is not seen or heard from directly at all. But believers like Esther still trusted in him and sought his help in prayer. The Lord's guardian care is powerfully evident throughout the book. Though unseen, Israel's keeper was not sleeping, but worked out a mighty salvation for his afflicted people. Those who believed were able to rely on him, assured of his watchful care. Like Esther and the Lord's faithful people of her generation, we may be called upon to walk through dark times or places, not knowing what lies ahead. But we may still be confident that our God is guarding us like a sentry round the camp.

The next stanza, verses 5–6, refers to God as a shade or covering: 'The LORD is your keeper; the LORD is your shade on your right hand. The sun shall not strike you by day, nor the moon by night.' The danger from the sun's harsh rays is obvious. The reference to the moon may be connected to the popular ancient belief that its rays were spiritually harmful. The word *lunatic* derives from *luna*, the Latin word for the moon.

The teaching here is that God cares for his people by shielding them as they travel. This may recall the time of the Exodus, when for many years the Israelites journeyed through the harsh desert environment. God was teaching them to depend on him for everything. Their food was the manna he sent from heaven. The Lord provided water for his thirsty people from the flinty rocks. The pillar of cloud by day and the pillar of fire by night were always present with them. It showed them when to move and where to go. When it stopped, they stopped; when it moved, they moved. This was their life of faith – an excellent example for us – a people ready to follow as and when God directed. In the heat of day the cloud spread out above them as a canopy over their heads – a shade to comfort and protect.

The Sinai desert is one of the most hostile climates on earth. During the day the temperatures climb to well over 100 degrees; when darkness falls it may plunge to below freezing. God sent his people to pass through this hostile environment. Likewise, he leads us through this wilderness-world before our entry into the Promised Land of heaven. In biblical terms, this present life is not a playground but a spiritual wasteland; if God should not provide for us and shield us we would surely perish. In this way he teaches us to trust him, to draw near to him and receive all our help at his hand. As in the days of Israel's ancient history, so today the Lord is 'your shade on your right hand. The sun shall not strike you by day, nor the moon by night.'

The final stanza sums this all up: 'The LORD will keep you from all evil; he will keep your life. The LORD will keep your going out and your coming in from this time forth and for evermore' (verses 7–8). Every kind of danger and hardship comes to us under God's guardian eye. Throughout the whole of our life, in all our coming and going, the Lord is ready at hand to ensure that no real harm comes to us.

Do you believe this? Do you think this is a claim we can credibly make today? Do these assurances square up with the experience of life as we know it? Understand that this psalm does not promise us an absence of troubles, but rather assumes them. From the beginning it acknowledges our need for help: 'Where does my help come from?' Ours is a difficult life and Christians cannot bypass the troubles endemic to a fallen world of sin. We may get sick and may suffer pain. We may have unsympathetic bosses and may suddenly lose our jobs. We may be slandered and robbed and otherwise victimized. There will be, as Jesus said, 'wars and rumours of wars . . . nation will rise against nation, and kingdom against kingdom, and there will be famines and earthquakes in various places' (*Matt.* 24:6–7). There will be heresies and divisions in the church. Persecution will come and we ourselves will sin against one another. We will struggle and experience sorrow and, should the Lord tarry, each of us will suffer death.

How, then, can the claims of this psalm be a comfort to us? The answer is that while all of the above is true, none of these things will really do any harm to the one who trusts in God. Why? Because God himself is our guardian and in love he watches over us to 'keep us from all evil'. I think the Apostle Paul put this best in Romans 8:37–39, where he catalogues every kind of possible harm but proceeds to assure us that we cannot be separated from God's saving love:

> In all these things we are more than conquerors through him who loved us. For I am sure that neither death nor life, nor angels nor rulers, nor things present nor things to come, nor powers, nor height nor depth, nor anything else in all creation, will be able to separate us from the love of God in Christ Jesus our Lord.

If you have lifted your eyes and looked up to the hills but have then realized that only God can deliver you, and that he has sent Jesus Christ to be your Saviour in whom you now trust, then you should not permit yourself to doubt the claims of this great psalm. Jesus Christ died for us; he gave his own blood to save us from death and hell and to secure us for himself. Surely, the sacrificial, sin-atoning death of the Son of God will not fail to accomplish all the gracious, saving purposes for which the Father designed it and for which the Son made it! Hebrews 7:25 says of Christ, 'He is *able* to save to the uttermost those who draw near to God through him, since he always lives to make intercession for them.' Moreover, when Jesus ascended into heaven he entered into his present priestly ministry that further guarantees our safety. Jesus is the guardian of this psalm, the Saviour and Lord who watches over our lives and preserves us.

This connects us again to the theme of the Lord as our shepherd, in which Psalm 23 so eloquently rejoices. This is one of the great themes of Scripture. Indeed, Jesus' great teaching about the Good Shepherd in John chapter 10 most clearly connects with our theme of God's guardian help. Psalm 121 says, 'The LORD will keep your going out and your coming in.' Jesus said, 'I am the door. If anyone enters by me, he will be saved and will go in and out and find pasture.' He was echoing the themes of this psalm, and relating these themes to himself as our shepherd. Yes, you will have trouble, but of all who look to him in faith, he says, 'My sheep hear my voice, and I know them, and they follow me. I give them eternal life, and they will never perish, and no one will snatch them out of my hand' (*John* 10:27–28).

Watching Over Your Life

I mentioned that Psalm 121 is a favourite passage for funeral services. I like to use its final verses to make a comforting point about the Christian's hope in death as in life. Verses 7 and 8 say, 'The LORD will keep you from all evil; he will keep your life. The LORD will keep your going out and your coming in from this time forth and for evermore.' Notice that God's guardian care is both now and 'for evermore'. It does not end with death; 'for evermore' he watches over 'your life'.

Many times I have stood over the cold ground of a Christian's grave, reading these verses, then commenting that God still watches over the life of the dear departed believer. The body is dead, but the Christian is alive and with the Lord. His soul lives and God watches over that precious soul until the great coming day when the trumpet will sound. Even in death, all who trust in Christ will be kept safe by God until the great resurrection morning.

What an incentive to trust him, both for life and for death, in our coming and in our going! If you call upon the Lord Jesus Christ, you will find him a vigilant protector. Certainly, there will be rocky paths, but your feet will not slip. There will be darkness on the way, but God will neither slumber nor sleep in his care over you. The sun will beat down; scorching trials and troubles will come. Like on a moonlit night there will be dark shadows cast across your path. But God will be close at hand to shade you from all harm. 'The LORD will keep you from all evil.' 'In the world you will have tribulation', Jesus foretold. 'But take heart; I have overcome the world' (*John* 16:33).

What a comfort this is to struggling believers! Will you make it to the end? Will your faith endure? You look to yourself, to the weakness of your faith, to the power of sin and temptation, and the future looks bleak indeed. But the Psalmist says, 'The LORD will keep you from all evil . . . He will keep your going out and your coming in from this time forth and for evermore.' The Lord guards you, morning and evening, now and forever. Encouraged by his guardian care, we should trust him in all our troubles and commit ourselves to doing his will.

Have you trusted in the Lord Jesus Christ? For the believer, there is life even in death, for God will watch over your life; he will keep your life, he will guard and protect your soul. Jesus said, 'I am the resurrection and the life. Whoever believes in me, though he die, yet shall he live, and everyone who lives and believes in me shall never die. Do you believe this?' (*John* 11:25–26).

5

HOW TO PRAISE THE LORD (PART 1)
PSALM 103:1–5

Bless the LORD, O my soul, and all that is within me, bless his holy name! Bless the LORD, O my soul, and forget not all his benefits (*Psa.* 103:1–2).

In his book, *Disappointment with God*,[1] best-selling author Philip Yancey writes about a number of letters he received from Christians who had expressed the sentiment found in his title. They had believed in God, but things did not work out as they had thought they would. So they were disappointed with God. One had suffered by seeing his parents divorce despite praying a thousand times for their reconciliation. Another had lost a child. Yet another just wasn't able to be happy, and God didn't seem to care. Instead of praising God they doubted him, rejected him, even hated him.

Yancey points out that many of these people were disappointed because they were trusting God for things he had never promised – namely, to preserve them from all pain and sorrow in this present life. Furthermore, he notes, even when people do get what they want, they usually fail to praise and thank God in

[1] Grand Rapids: Zondervan, 1988.

response. In times of plenty and in want, in joy and in sorrow, our souls need to be stirred up to praise the Lord.

Bless the LORD, O My Soul

This is exactly what King David found to be true of his own soul. Psalm 103 begins and ends with David exhorting his inner self to praise the Lord: 'Bless the LORD, O my soul', he writes. In between, he gives reasons why his soul should offer this praise. It is often said today that what we need is heart religion, and with this David surely agrees. He wants praise to come from his soul, from his innermost being. It is not enough for him to praise the Lord merely with his feet by coming to church, or merely with his mouth by speaking and singing. He knows that God rejects worship that is only outward and from hearts that are far from him (see *Isa.* 29:13). David would have agreed that what we need today is heart religion.

However, many people say that what gets in the way of heart religion is head religion, and to this David would have strenuously objected. Certainly, there are people whose 'faith' is merely a lifeless intellectualism; that is not genuine faith. But Psalm 103 demonstrates clearly just how much the heart depends upon the mind; it is the light of God's truth shining from his instructed mind that warms David's otherwise reluctant heart. Here we see David reasoning with his heart. He is preaching a sermon to his own soul, which is something we frequently have cause to do. He reminds himself of truths that he expects will cause his heart to rise in warm and fervent praise to God.

We have reached a point of transition in our study of the Christian life as depicted through the lens of the Psalms. The first four chapters of this book were given to describing our relationship with God and the attitude we ought to have toward him. The remainder of the book will consider the fruits of this relationship. Primary among these is a heart that is eager to worship. God created and redeemed us to glorify and praise his Name.

It is hard to underestimate the importance of having a heart that praises the Lord. David knew that his own spiritual life grew strong through an attitude of praise to God. He knew that hardness of heart caused Israel to be unfaithful to the Lord. With this in mind, David implores, as should we, 'Bless the LORD, O my soul, and all that is within me, bless his holy name!'

Forget Not All His Benefits

Psalm 103 can be divided into three sections; in each section David seeks to praise God from the depths of his being. Verses 1 to 5 speak of gratitude to God for his blessings; verses 6 to 14 speak of love to God in response to his love for us; and verses 15 to 22 conclude with a feeling of awe on account of God's greatness and glory.

David stirs his heart to gratitude by calling to mind all that God has done for him. 'Bless the LORD, O my soul', he says, 'and forget not all his benefits.' If the question is, 'How are we to praise the Lord?' his first answer is that we praise the Lord when we gratefully remember how God has savingly blessed us. True gratitude is one of the most powerful of all motivations; it is thanksgiving that causes us to live in praise of God. Therefore the words of verse 2 ought to be frequently placed before every Christian's heart: 'Bless the LORD, O my soul, and forget not all his benefits.' Our problem is that we do forget; it is the believer who has a fresh appreciation of what God has done in Jesus Christ who is glad and longs to glorify God.

To this end, David works through a catalogue of the benefits for which he is thankful, counting his blessings in a chain of God's grace. It is surely significant that the first of these is the forgiveness of sin. 'Bless the LORD', he says, 'who forgives all your iniquity' (verse 3).

There are so many things for which we ought to praise the Lord – our homes and jobs, our wealth and health. But none of these compare to the forgiveness of our sins, for what is all the world worth if we should lose our own souls? If the psalm came to an end in verse 3 we would have ample reason to praise the Lord eternally; we can know the forgiveness of our sins only because God, in his great love for us, gave his Son to bear on the cross the punishment our sins deserved.

This shows us that only those who remember their sins will really praise the Lord with thanksgiving. It is only when we realize the magnitude of our guilt, the enormity of the offence our sin has given to God's holy justice, that God's grace seems so wonderful and worthy of our praise. This is one reason why we should regularly confess our sins; it leads to heartfelt gratitude for God's forgiving mercy. If we are disappointed with God, it is certain that we have forgotten what our sins deserve from him, namely, condemnation and wrath. But when we remember that God has forgiven us, and at such great cost to himself – the incarnation, sufferings, and atoning death of his beloved Son – how can we ever again speak of being disappointed with God?

As great as forgiveness is, it is but the beginning of the benefits the believer enjoys. If you are a recent convert, full of the joy of sins forgiven, then you will be very interested to discover the other benefits David describes here. If you have been a Christian for some time, then these are blessings with which you should be increasingly familiar.

With *forgiveness*, David pairs *healing:* 'Who forgives all your iniquity; who heals all your diseases' (verse 3). Since David is addressing his soul we should think of this mainly as spiritual healing, for sin leads not only to guilt that needs to be forgiven but also to inner corruption that needs to be healed. This is what Augustus Toplady expressed so succinctly in the great lines of his hymn *Rock of Ages:*

> Be of sin the double cure,
> Cleanse me from its guilt and power.

So many of Jesus' miracles involved cleansing and healing – we especially remember his healing and cleansing of the lepers.

The Lord's miracles were more than 'mighty works'; they were signs pointing to spiritual truth. In saving sinners, Jesus Christ works a progressive and powerful cleansing of our thought, attitude, and desire. What a cause for grateful praise! Jesus makes the sinner whole! In the end, all our diseases, of body and soul, will be healed in the resurrection. What else can we say but, 'Bless the LORD, O my soul'!

To this David adds a third benefit: 'Who redeems your life from the pit' (verse 4). Whenever I read these words I think of John Newton, who for many years was given over to sin as a brutal slave trader. During a voyage home to England his ship was caught up in a savage storm. Terrified, Newton worked a pump in the darkness of his ship's hold for hours on end, over several days. In that darkness, he remembered a Bible verse his godly mother had taught him many years before in his childhood. There and then, he cried to God to save him. Alone in the dark hold of the ship he was converted. God saved him not only from the danger of that storm but from the dark pit of his vile and sinful life. His gratitude to God found expression in his best-known hymn:

> Amazing grace! (how sweet the sound!)
>   That saved a wretch like me;
> I once was lost, but now am found;
>   Was blind, but now I see.

Forgiveness speaks of pardon from sin's guilt; healing speaks of cleansing from sin's corrupting power; *redemption* tells of deliverance from the misery into which sin has cast us. For some it is the bondage of an addiction or a lifestyle of gross sin. For others it is abuse, or persecution, or illness. We may have known the more subtle but no less dangerous slaveries of anger, greed, lust, and pride. But God redeems us out of all these horrible pits.

Ultimately, David's reference is to the pit of death. Death is the enemy we all will face, and God will redeem our bodies from the pit of the grave and share with us the blessings of Christ's glorious resurrection. 'Bless the LORD, O my soul!'

This, too, is coupled with a corresponding blessing: 'Who crowns you with steadfast love and mercy' (verse 4). We don't often think of being *crowned*, do we? The idea associated with crowning is the bestowal of dignity and honour. Far better than the gold that crowns earthly kings are the love and mercy God bestows on us. God's love and mercy are precious jewels that shine more brightly than diamonds in settings of pure gold. David puts these blessings together to show that while sin has dragged us down to the pit, salvation elevates us to the highest honour by making us the heirs of God.

Jesus depicted this in his parable of the prodigal son. Having scorned his father and wasted his money, the prodigal found himself in the greatest misery. So low had he sunk that he would have gladly filled his stomach with the food of the pigs he was hired to tend. What an accurate picture of the life of sin and how it dehumanizes the sinner! The memory of his father's goodness and love brought him to his senses, and he set out for home. Having cast away his sonship he longed to return to his father's house as a servant. But, in the prodigal son's repentant return, Jesus presents a matchless picture of our heavenly Father's crowning grace. 'The father said to his servants "Bring quickly the best robe, and put it on him, and put a ring on his hand, and shoes on his feet . . . For this my son was dead, and is alive again; he was lost, and is found"' (*Luke* 15:22–24). The best robe signifies the imputed righteousness in Christ, the ring is a symbol of honour and authority, such as Joseph received as Pharaoh's deputy, and the shoes speak of sonship in a world where slaves walked barefoot. Like the prodigal, we too have suffered misery because of sin and have merited rejection, but when we return to God he crowns us with steadfast love and mercy. 'Bless the LORD, O my soul!'

Verse 5 completes David's catalogue of saving benefits: 'Who satisfies you with good so that your youth is renewed like the eagle's.' *Satisfaction* is a word we seldom hear today. The Rolling Stones spoke for their whole generation when they sang, 'I can't get no satisfaction.' We are a people who are satiated with pleasure, much of it sinful, and yet we feel so dissatisfied. We have all that we want and very little of what we need to make us truly happy.

God offers not satiation but satisfaction: 'He satisfies my desires', David says (verse 5, NIV). We remember that David is addressing his soul; it is the soul that God, and only God, satisfies. Psalm 37:4 says, 'Delight yourself in the LORD, and he will give you the desires of your heart.' What good news that is to a generation like ours! If you walk with God he will satisfy your soul. That is what Jesus said to the Samaritan woman at Jacob's well, 'Whoever drinks of the water that I will give him will never be thirsty again. The water that I will give him will become in him a spring of water welling up to eternal life' (*John* 4:14). 'Sir,' the woman replied, 'give me this water.' God will give soul-satisfying eternal life to all who repent of their sins and come to Christ in faith.

That does not mean that Christians will never experience hardship, sickness, poverty, or pain. Nor will it mean that all our worldly wants will be instantly fulfilled. Jesus said, 'If anyone would come after me, let him deny himself and take up his cross daily and follow me' (*Luke* 9:23). But he also said, 'Truly, I say to you, there is no one who has left house or wife or brothers or parents or children, for the sake of the kingdom of God, who will not receive many times more in this time, and in the age to come eternal life' (*Luke* 18:29–30). 'Bless the LORD, O my soul!'

Finally, David says that our youth will be '*renewed* like the eagle's'. This is similar to what Paul says about the Christian's inward renewal: 'Though our outer nature is wasting away, our inner nature is being renewed day by day' (*2 Cor.* 4:16). The eagle is a symbol of strength and vigour, and God gives these to the trusting soul.

This is especially fulfilled in the life beyond death. I think of the last words of the nineteenth-century preacher, Dr Edward Payson, dying in the midst of great pain. This is the Christian's testimony at death: He said, 'I *know* that my happiness is but begun. It will last forever . . . It seems as if my soul had found a pair of new wings and is so eager to try them.'[2] Isaiah likewise said: 'They who wait for the LORD shall renew their strength; they shall mount up with wings like eagles; they shall run and not be weary; they shall walk and not faint.' (*Isa.* 40:31). With this, David completes his chain of benefits for which his soul should praise the Lord.

This, then, is the first way we learn to praise the Lord, through gratitude for his saving benefits. Something that happened shortly after the end of the American Civil War provides us with a wonderful illustration of such gratitude. A man in farm clothes was seen kneeling at a gravestone in the soldiers' cemetery in Nashville. An observer came up and asked, 'Is that the grave of your son?' The farmer replied, 'No, I have seven children, all of them young, and a wife on my poor farm in Illinois. I was drafted and, despite the great hardship it would cause, I was required to join the Army. But on the morning I was to depart this man, my neighbour's older son, came over and offered to take my place in the war.' The observer solemnly asked, 'What is that you are writing on his grave?' The farmer replied, 'I am writing, "He died for me."'

If that is how a man naturally feels for the son of his fellow man who took his place and died in his stead – so that he holds his name precious all the days of his life – how much more ought our gratitude to cause us to praise the Lord! God's own Son came down from heaven and took up our flesh. He lived and toiled for us. He entered the battle of sin on our behalf, though he was himself exempt from it. He died in our place, suffering the wrath of God that we might be forgiven. Not only that, he

[2] Quoted in Murdoch Campbell, *From Grace to Glory: Meditations on the Book of Psalms* (London: Banner of Truth, 1970), p. 154.

rose from the grave to crown us with all the blessings of heaven, to give us a future in glory and a place in the renewal of all things. Do you believe that? If you do, you surely ought to plead, 'Bless the LORD, O my soul, and forget not all his benefits.' Here is a text we ought regularly to preach to our souls, that we might gratefully praise the Lord.

A Grateful Life That Blesses God

As Psalm 103 progresses, David gives his heart two more reasons to praise the Lord. But so important is this first reason – *gratitude* for salvation's blessings – that we should dwell on its implication for our lives. Specifically, gratitude for God's blessings not only causes our hearts to *praise* the Lord but also motivates us to *please* the Lord in the manner of our living.

David says, 'Bless the LORD, O my soul!' I have been translating *bless* as *praise*, and that is its main meaning in this context. But there is also the idea we perhaps most often think of in the word *bless*, namely to *please* or minister to the one we want to bless. Of course, this is linked with praise. David wants his soul to praise the Lord and he wants his soul to please the Lord; the two necessarily go together. Indeed, if we really want to praise the Lord it is not going to happen merely by coming to church and singing and sitting for an hour or so, but by living in a way that is inspired by God's grace and directed towards his pleasure.

This is an important matter to every Christian who wants to live in a way that pleases the Lord. The issue, therefore, of great concern to us is how to gain the necessary influence over our hearts – that is, over our desires and passions and affections – so that we may live in this way. I think one important answer is found in the opening section of Psalm 103 – by facing the reality of our *guilt* before God, by perceiving in faith the great gift of God's *grace*, and then by responding to him with a *gratitude* that wants to bless the Lord. *Guilt, grace,* and *gratitude* – that sums up the thought-processes of a heart that wants to bless the Lord.

One woman whose life was transformed by gratitude to God was Corrie ten Boom. Corrie was a young Dutch woman when the troops of Nazi Germany invaded Holland in 1940. Not long after the invasion, the Nazis began persecuting the Jewish people living there. Every Jew was issued with a bright yellow Star of David which had to be worn at all times. Corrie and her family were saddened by this, since as Christians they had always felt affection for these kinsmen of our Lord Jesus Christ. Before long, the ten Boom family was engaged in the dangerous business of hiding Jews from the Germans, as more and more Jewish people began to disappear or be taken away.

Corrie became involved in the Dutch underground, working hard to provide safe refuge and ration cards for a great many Jewish people. The ten Booms had a fake wall built in a room in their house to create a secret place in which they could hide Jews. From 1940 to 1944, the family safeguarded and helped numerous Jews escape from the Nazis, until they were betrayed. One morning in February 1944, members of the Gestapo, the Nazi secret police, burst into their house. Corrie and the other family members were beaten, but none would divulge the hiding place and the Jews who were there. Nonetheless, the whole family was arrested. That night Corrie's father led them in a prayer from Psalm 119, 'You are my hiding place and my shield: I hope in your word . . . Hold me up, and I shall be safe.'

The ten Booms were taken to a nearby prison and separated from one another. Soon Corrie's father died; she, herself, became ill. While at the hospital, one of the nurses secretly gave her little booklets containing the four Gospels. Corrie was sent back to her freezing cell, and though nearly starved to death she slowly regained strength. Finally, her time of interrogation came, during which Corrie feared she would betray her friends under torture. 'Lord Jesus,' she prayed, 'You were once questioned too. Please show me what to do.' During her interrogation, Corrie was not tortured and even found the boldness to tell her Nazi captor about the love of God through Jesus Christ. During the second session, the Nazi officer admitted that he hated his work and feared for his family back in Germany, and asked would she tell him again about the forgiveness and peace God offers through Jesus, his Son.

In the months to come that officer was able to help Corrie, although he was unable to set her free. Alone in her cell, reading her Gospels over and over, Corrie reflected on the death of Christ and God's ability to turn suffering into victory. After the Allied invasion of Normandy, the prisoners were moved to Germany and things became more brutal than ever. On one single day, Corrie witnessed the execution of seven hundred prisoners. She was exposed to forced labour and savage beatings, with almost nothing given her to eat. In this terrible place, Corrie and her sister Betsie, with whom she had been reunited, started a Bible study in the overcrowded cell they shared. One biographer writes, 'Under these terrible conditions, the goodness in the words of the Bible shone out brightly and their message of God's love brought comfort. With death all around, the promise of eternal life and the glory of heaven gave the women hope for the future.'[3]

On one occasion, Corrie watched Betsie being beaten while praying for her tormentors. Betsie became ill and began to falter, and in spite of Corrie's care and attention died. A few days later, Corrie heard her own name called out during a roll-call. Certain that she was summoned for execution, she prayed for God's help. To her astonishment she was given a card marked 'Released'. She was given back her possessions, some new clothes and a railway pass to Holland. Later she found out that her release had been an administrative mistake and that a week afterwards all the women in her cell were put to death.

I tell this story not simply because of its fascinating details but to make a point. Here was a woman who suffered enormously, who experienced tragedies that would embitter

[3] David Wallington, 'The Secret Room: The Story of Corrie ten Boom,' *SOON Online Magazine* at http: //www.soon.org. uk.

most peoples' souls. Corrie did struggle with anger and bitterness. After the war ended, she wrote an angry letter to the man whose informing had led to her family's arrest, telling him of their suffering on account of his act of betrayal. But she also found grace to tell him of how God had helped her and how he could be saved by turning in repentance and faith to Christ. She concluded the letter by writing that God was helping her to forgive him and that she would pray for his salvation. Days later, the man was executed by the Dutch authorities.

Corrie began telling people about God's love and the miraculous way he had saved her. She established a home for people who had suffered during the war, as well as a camp for former prisoners and refugees. Because of her remarkable experiences, only a few of which I have shared, she received invitations to speak in many places and she began to write books.

Following one of these speaking engagements the defining moment in Corrie ten Boom's life arrived. This is how she tells the story:

> It was at a church service in Munich that I saw him, the former S.S. man who had stood guard at the shower room door in the processing centre at Ravensbruck. He was the first of our actual jailors that I had seen since that time. And suddenly it was all there – the roomful of mocking men, the heaps of clothing, Betsie's pain-blanched face.
>
> He came up to me as the church was emptying, beaming and bowing, 'How grateful I am for your message, Fraulein', he said. 'To think that, as you say, He has washed my sins away!'
>
> His hand was thrust out to shake mine. And I, who had preached so often . . . the need to forgive, kept my hand at my side.
>
> Even as the angry, vengeful thoughts boiled through me, I saw the sin of them. Jesus Christ had died for this man; was I going to ask for more? Lord Jesus, I prayed, forgive me and help me to forgive him.
>
> I tried to smile, I struggled to raise my hand. I could not. I felt nothing, not the slightest spark of warmth or charity. And so again

I breathed a silent prayer. Jesus, I cannot forgive him. Give me Your forgiveness.

As I took his hand the most incredible thing happened. From my shoulder along my arm and through my hand a current seemed to pass from me to him, while into my heart sprang a love for this stranger that almost overwhelmed me.[4]

With tears in her eyes, she thrust her hand into his and said, 'I forgive you, brother.' For a long moment they grasped each other's hand, the former guard and the former prisoner, the former tormentor and the former victim. How can you explain that? Corrie later did, saying, 'There is no pit so deep that God's love is not deeper still.'

'Bless the LORD, O my soul,' David writes, 'and forget not all his benefits.' That is not just for famous or special Christians. It is for all of us. It is for you. Corrie ten Boom remembered all that God had done for her and it changed her heart. Like her, we can look at this catalogue of blessings David writes about in Psalm 103, and we can be grateful for what God has done and is doing for us. He heals our souls, he redeems us from the pits into which our sin and the sins of others have cast us. He crowns us with mercy and love, he satisfies our souls with spiritual delights; he promises an eternity in glory and our youth renewed like the eagle's. But most of all, and surely it was remembering this that most enabled Corrie ten Boom to forgive a man who had tormented her so greatly, God has forgiven our sins at so great a cost to himself.

We need to remember these things. We need to meditate on these verses and pray for God to fill our hearts with gratitude and praise. And if we do that, surely there will be a difference in our lives; surely we will long to bless the Lord who has blessed us so much in Christ, and it will change the way that we think and speak and act. 'Bless the LORD, O my soul, and all that is within me, bless his holy name!'

[4] Corrie ten Boom, *The Hiding Place* (Grand Rapids: Baker, 1984), p. 215.

6

HOW TO PRAISE THE LORD (PART 2)
PSALM 103:6–22

The LORD is merciful and gracious, slow to anger and abounding in steadfast love (*Psa.* 103:8).

In the last chapter we looked at the first part of Psalm 103, in which King David seeks to motivate his heart to praise the Lord. 'Bless the LORD, O my soul,' he urges. In verses 2–5, we saw the powerful role gratitude plays in stirring up praise to God. 'Forget not all his benefits', David writes, and he follows that up with an impressive recounting of the blessings for which every Christian should gratefully praise the Lord: *forgiveness, healing, redemption, crowning, satisfaction,* and *renewal.* If we really want to live for the glory of God, then we will exercise our hearts with this kind of remembrance; we will read and meditate and pray with the aim of becoming increasingly grateful for all that God has done for us.

The remainder of Psalm 103 focuses on two other motivations to live in praise of God, namely, *love* for him and *awe* for his greatness and majesty. Recently I read a fine book on Christian spirituality in which the author stressed that a balanced spiritual life will possess both of these elements. To be balanced in our walk with God we need both to love and to fear him. The author, Jerry Bridges, said this: 'To seek to grow in the fear of God . . . without also growing in our comprehension of His love can cause us to begin to view God as far-off and austere. Or to seek to grow in our awareness of the love of God without also growing in our reverence and awe of Him can cause us to view God as a permissive and indulgent heavenly Father who does not deal with our sin.'[1] By that standard, David strikes a perfect balance in Psalm 103:6–22, presenting his soul with ample reasons both to love God and to hold him in reverential fear.

Love for the God of Love

First, let us consider David's marvellous depiction of God's saving love for us in verses 6–14, a picture that is calculated to cause his and our hearts to respond with love for God in return.

Verse 8 is the key to this section: 'The LORD is merciful and gracious, slow to anger and abounding in steadfast love.' David gathers together various words that are guaranteed to lift our hearts in praise. These are the wellsprings of God's love from which flow our whole salvation: from God's mercy we receive pardon; from his grace we receive favour; from the Lord's long-suffering comes his patience; and from God's steadfast love flows his bountiful kindness. If only David's heart can comprehend something of the greatness of the compassion and love of God, and can grasp the beauty of his lovingkindness, his heart will surely echo with love for God in return.

In verses 6–14, David develops his case for God's love: first, he *proves* God's love. David wrote this psalm ten centuries before the coming of Christ. In his day the great episode of redemption was the Exodus of Israel from Egypt. David, therefore, turns to this as a sure *proof* of God's love: 'The LORD works righteousness and justice for all who are oppressed. He made known his ways to Moses, his acts to the people of Israel'

---

[1] Jerry Bridges, *The Practice of Godliness* (Colorado Springs: NavPress, 1996), p. 47.

(verses 6–7). In the Exodus, God provided justice for his people by breaking the bonds of their captivity and leading them to freedom in the Promised Land. More importantly, God provided a way of atonement for his people, through the sacrifices ordained in the law. These sacrifices pointed ultimately to the cross of Jesus Christ. God also gave his Word, so that his redeemed would know his ways and be his distinctive holy people.

Through the Exodus deliverance, David saw a wonderful proof of God's love for his people. This is what Moses himself stressed in Deuteronomy 7:7–8, 'It was not because you were more in number than any other people that the LORD set his love on you and chose you, for you were the fewest of all peoples, but it is because the LORD loves you . . . that the LORD has brought you out with a mighty hand and redeemed you from the house of slavery, from the hand of Pharaoh king of Egypt.' The Exodus proved God's love for his people and it called for their love to him in return. Deuteronomy 6:5 said, 'You shall love the LORD your God with all your heart and with all your soul and with all your might' (*Deut.* 6:5). Jesus referred to this as the first and greatest commandment.

If David in his time looked back to the Exodus and saw in it a great proof of God's love that called for love to God in return, then what must Christians say about the cross of our Lord Jesus Christ? Surely this is the greatest of all proofs of God's love for a wayward world! The Puritan Jeremiah Burroughs wrote of the cross:

> Behold the infinite love of God to mankind and the love of Jesus Christ that, rather than God see the children of men to perish eternally, would send His Son to take our nature upon Him and thus suffer such dreadful things. Herein God shows His love . . . It pleased the Father to break His Son and to pour out His blood. Here is the love of God and of Jesus Christ. Oh, what a powerful, mighty, drawing, efficacious meditation this should be to us![2]

---

[2] *Gospel Worship* (Morgan, PA: Soli Deo Gloria, 1990), p. 353.

That is exactly David's own line of reasoning. It is also the reasoning found in New Testament passages like Romans 5:8, where Paul writes that God proved his love for us 'in that while we were still sinners, Christ died for us'. How can you doubt the love of someone who willingly dies in your place? This is what God has done for you in the person of his Son, Jesus Christ. How can we doubt his supreme affection for us even amidst the greatest trials? How can we fail to love him in return?

In verses 9 and 10 we have, in the second place, the greatest *display* of God's love in the way he reacts to our sin. David writes, 'He will not always chide, nor will he keep his anger forever. He does not deal with us according to our sins, nor repay us according to our iniquities.' The very fact that God placed us on this green earth, that he causes the sun to shine and the rain to fall, proves his love for us. But the greatest display of his love is seen in his response to our sin. On the one hand, God is angry when we sin, and he seeks to convict our hearts of the wrong we have done against him. But God does not berate us constantly, nor does he harbour grudges.

According only to his justice, God would punish us on account of our sin. But, 'He does not deal with us according to our sins.' What can explain such divine treatment toward sinners? The love of God. Many Christians are depressed by an awareness of their own sin, because they assume that God will turn against them. But our awareness of sin should lead us to praise God for his loving mercy toward us. What a display of love this is: 'He does not repay us according to our iniquities.' 'God shows his love for us in that while we were still sinners, Christ died for us' (*Rom.* 5:8). 'Bless the LORD, O my soul!'

Verses 11 and 12 are among the best loved in all the Psalms. They present the *measure* of God's love. Verse 11 says, 'For as high as the heavens are above the earth, so great is his steadfast love toward those who fear him.' God's love is infinite – beyond measure or calculation. There was a famous incident many years ago when the first Russian cosmonaut broke through into space.

Being an atheist, he announced mockingly to all the world, 'I have entered heaven but I don't see any God here.' In light of this verse, he should have cried, 'Having entered into space I see that there is an infinite distance to the heavens. According to the Bible, as high as this measureless span of heaven is, so great is God's love for those who trust him.' Think of the star in the night, twinkling at you from so vast a distance. There is a God who made that star, who says that his love for you extends far beyond that measure. 'Bless the Lord, O my soul!'

Verse 12 applies this directly to the crucial matter of forgiveness of sin: 'As far as the east is from the west, so far does he remove our transgressions from us.' How often anxious thoughts arise in our hearts about the extent to which God forgives our sin. We know only too well how difficult it is for us to forgive others for what they have done to us, and we suspect the same must be true for God. But look here at what God has written. The east is the farthest thing from the west and yet God has removed our sins from us as far as the east is from the west! This is the measure of God's love for his people.

This truth was dramatized in Old Testament Israel by one of the rites that took place on the Day of Atonement, as explained in Leviticus 16. The high priest took two goats, one of which was sacrificed, symbolizing the blood of Christ to atone for our sins. The other was called the scapegoat. On this goat the priest laid his hands, symbolically transferring the sins of all the people to the animal. The scapegoat then was led out to a distant place where it was released, disappearing from the peoples' sight forever. Whereas the first goat that died symbolized Christ's atoning blood, the second goat or scapegoat symbolized what happened to our sins. 'As far as the east is from the west, so far has he removed our transgressions from us.'

This means that when you confess your sins and come to God for cleansing through Jesus Christ, you will never hear about those sins from him again. Those sins, all of those sins, are gone. They will not hang over your head to embitter your relationship with him, the way so many human relationships are sadly embittered by unforgiven sins. As soon as our sins are confessed and forgiven they no longer stand in the way of our communion with the God of love, for he has said, 'I will be merciful towards their iniquities, and I will remember their sins no more' (*Heb.* 8:12).

When we think of the measure of God's love, we sometimes think of the outstretched arms of Jesus' arms upon the cross. J. I. Packer adds:

> The measure of love is how much it gives, and the measure of the love of God is the gift of His only Son to be made man, and to die for sins, and so to become the one Mediator who can bring us to God. No wonder Paul speaks of God's love as 'great', and passing knowledge! (*Eph.* 2:4; 3:19). Was there ever such costly munificence?[3]

'Bless the LORD, O my soul!'

Verses 13–14 complete David's presentation with an *illustration* of God's love: 'As a father shows compassion to his children, so the LORD shows compassion to those who fear him. For he knows our frame; he remembers that we are dust.' Fathers feel for their children with a loving empathy. Remember Jesus' portrayal of the love of the father in the parable of the prodigal son? Henry Lyte's great hymn on our text says,

> Father-like, he tends and spares us;
> Well our feeble frame he knows;
> In his hands he gently bears us,
> Rescues us from all our foes.[4]

Because of this love that David has proved, displayed, measured, and illustrated, surely our hearts will love him in return.

In the previous chapter I mentioned Philip Yancey's book *Disappointment with God*. In it Yancey reveals that when he

---

[3] J. I. Packer: *Knowing God* (Downers Grove: InterVarsity, 1979), p. 114.
[4] Henry F. Lyte, *Praise, My Soul, the King of Heaven*, 1834.

was just a baby his father died of polio. He grew up without a father and never really felt a father's love. Years later, Yancey found at his mother's house a crumpled photo of himself as a baby. He asked her why she held on to such a mangled picture when she had others that were so much better. She explained that this was the photo she had wedged inside the iron lung that encased his father during his dying weeks. She told of how his father spent his last months gazing upon this photograph, praying for his upbringing, delighting in just a picture of his son. Yancey writes, 'Someone I have no memory of . . . spent all day every day thinking of me, devoting himself to me, loving me as well as he could.'[5] That is how a father loves, and it is but an illustration of the great love that fills our heavenly Father's heart. 'Bless the LORD, O my soul!'

If you have never come to this God of love for salvation, then I would ask you to think about the love you are rejecting – the love of a father. Do you not yearn for such a love?

We are all trained to seek love by trying to make ourselves lovely or lovable. This is the way the world thinks; if we want to be loved – and we do – then we have to earn that love. The result is a performance mentality that offers no real peace or lasting joy, for the simple reason that we are always fearfully aware of how unlovable we really are. How can God really love me? But the Bible says God loves us because of a great love within himself. 'God is love', John says. 'In this the love of God was made manifest among us, that God sent his only Son into the world, so that we might live through him. In this is love, not that we have loved God but that he loved us and sent his Son to be the propitiation for our sins' (*1 John* 4:8–10). Therefore, he adds, 'We know and rely on the love God has for us' (*1 John* 4:16, NIV). 'There is no fear in love, but perfect love casts out fear' (*1 John* 4:18). And, finally, 'We love because he first loved us' (*1 John* 4:19). Our hope for love does not rest

---

[5] Philip Yancey, *Disappointment with God*, p. 255.

on something worth loving in us, but instead rests on the great, conquering love that is in God. The only thing for us to do is to love God in return. 'Bless the LORD, O my soul!'

If you want to love God as you ought, then you must start by believing how great his love for you in Jesus Christ is. When that happens you will show your love for God by thinking about him, by reading and obeying his love letter (that is, the Bible), by serving him with joy, and by having a special love for all your fellow believers – the dearly loved children of your heavenly Father.

Awe for God's Greatness and Glory

How shall we praise the Lord? First, there is gratitude for blessings received, in verses 1–5. Second, there is adoring love in response to God's perfect love for us, in verses 6–14. Third, in verses 15–19, David worships the Lord with *a sense of awe* for his greatness and glory.

In verses 15–16, David shows that praise for men is tragically misplaced: 'As for man, his days are like grass; he flourishes like a flower of the field; for the wind passes over it, and it is gone, and its place knows it no more.' But God is infinite; his love has no beginning and no end. God loved his people before they were created, and his unchanging and unchangeable love endures forever. David says, 'The steadfast love of the LORD is from everlasting to everlasting on those who fear him, and his righteousness to children's children, to those who keep his covenant and remember to do his commandments' (verses 17–18).

> Frail as summer's flower we flourish,
> Blows the wind and it is gone;
> But while mortals rise and perish,
> God endures unchanging on.
> Praise him! Praise him!
> Praise him! Praise him!
> Praise the High Eternal One.

Finally, David exclaims, 'The LORD has established his throne in the heavens, and his kingdom rules over all' (verse 19). The very throne of heaven is established by his hand. Stephen Charnock writes, 'It is fixed, not tottering; it is an unmovable dominion; all the strugglings of men and devils cannot overturn it, not so much as shake it . . . His dominion, as himself, abides for ever. And as his counsel, so his authority, shall stand; and 'he will do all his pleasure' (*Isa.* 46:10).'[6]

This sense of awe before the greatness of God is surely the one thing above all else that we most need to recover today. Yes, we need gratitude to God for the benefits of salvation – it is hard to place anything ahead of that. And we need lovingly to adore God in response to his fatherly love for us. But is it not this that we have most lost today – a sense of the grandeur, greatness, and glory of God? Isn't this why so many Christians are bored with God? Yes, we have forgotten his benefits, and so feel disappointed by him. Yes, we have trivialized his love, and so our hearts remain cold and unmoved. But do we not need, above all else, to recover a sense of wonder and awe, to see God as David does in this psalm, enthroned on high and sovereign over all in his awesome majesty. Jerry Bridges writes:

> In our day we must begin to recover a sense of awe and profound reverence for God. We must begin to view him once again in the infinite majesty that alone belongs to Him who is the Creator and Supreme Ruler of the entire universe. There is an infinite gap in worth and dignity between God the Creator and man the creature, even though man has been created in the image of God. The fear of God is a heartfelt recognition of this gap – not a putdown of man, but an exaltation of God.[7]

What a difference this attitude would make! Think of how it would transform our devotional lives. Instead of looking to get 'a little something' to help us through the day, we would come

---

[6] Stephen Charnock, quoted in Spurgeon, *A Treasury of David*, 3 vols. (Peabody: Hendrickson, n.d.), vol. 2, p. 295.
[7] Bridges, *Practice of Godliness*, p. 21.

to the awesome God primarily to worship him for his own sake. Think also of how it would transform our attitude when we gather for public worship. Instead of looking to leave church feeling good about ourselves, we would make it our chief end to please God according to his Word and to give glory to his Name. Moreover, think of how it would transform our attitude to the whole of life, both in the simplest and the greatest tasks we perform. To see God as holy and great ought to make us holy in all that we do and to make his pleasure the chief yardstick by which we measure everything.

Let Everybody Praise the Lord

I want to conclude with an observation and a question. First the observation. In his conclusion, David shows us that the heart that praises God seeks companions for worship. Those who praise the Lord want others to praise him, too. David searches high and low, calling out for all to praise the Lord:

> Bless the LORD, O you his angels, you mighty ones who do his word, obeying the voice of his word! Bless the LORD, all his hosts, his ministers, who do his will! Bless the LORD, all his works, in all places of his dominion (verses 20–22).

This shows us the link between worship and witness. If our hearts are gripped by the gospel, are inspired by gratitude and love and awe, then we will tell others about it. We will speak of salvation's blessings, of God's great forgiving love, of his majesty which is high above all earthly glory. And we will desire above all else to be present where God is truly praised, saying, as David does in conclusion, 'Bless the LORD, O my soul!'

Second, I have a question. Do you go to God's house with a genuine desire in your heart to praise the Lord? Or is it merely your lips that praise him? It is possible to appear to worship the Lord while the mind and especially the heart are far from him. But verse 17 says, 'The steadfast love of the LORD is . . . on those who fear him.' David is talking about those who glorify

God, who stand in awe of his majesty, and who place him first in the order of all things. Is that an accurate description of you?

A lukewarm spirituality is as dangerous today as it was in biblical times. Jesus gave a stern warning to the Laodiceans 'Because you are lukewarm, and neither hot nor cold, I will spit you out of my mouth' (*Rev.* 3:16). With that in mind, we, like David, need to apply God's Word to our hearts, so that we really will have a heart that praises the Lord. We need to count our blessings in Christ with thanksgiving; we need to look in gratitude to God for his boundless love toward us, and we need to kneel in awe before him, the great God and Lord of all. If you do that, then, by God's grace, your heart will respond in the same way that David's did, saying, 'Bless the LORD, O my soul, and all that is within me, bless his holy name!'

7

HOW TO PRAY
PSALM 5

Give ear to my words, O LORD; consider my groaning. Give attention to the sound of my cry for help, my King and my God, for to you I do pray' (*Psa.* 5:1–2).

In any study of the believer's communion with God, it is inevitable that we should find ourselves dealing with the subject of prayer. Prayer is the highest and most intimate expression of our relationship with God.

It is also no surprise that prayer is among those things most difficult to us. If it is generally true, as Paul puts it, that 'the flesh wars against the Spirit', it is especially true in the matter of prayer. This is why we find our hearts reluctant, our minds wandering, our zeal flagging when it comes to prayer. Since prayer is our greatest privilege on this side of heaven it is also the focal point of the most intense spiritual warfare.

I often advise those struggling in prayer to turn to the Book of Psalms, which God has given to lead us in prayer. The psalms are prayers inspired by the Holy Spirit, and we may find it useful to conclude our daily devotions by praying through one of the psalms.

All of the psalms are prayers, but Psalm 5 is especially valuable as a psalm specifically about prayer. We are not told the circumstances that gave rise to this psalm. It is considered by some to be a prayer for coming into God's house, but I think James Boice rightly describes it as 'a generic prayer showing how we must approach God, if we would be heard by him, and what we can expect of him when we do'.[1]

Prayer Is Coming to God

The first thing we are taught in this psalm is that *prayer is coming to God*. We see this clearly in the first stanza. Verses 1 and 2 say:

> Give ear to my words, O LORD, consider my groaning. Give attention to the sound of my cry, my King and my God, for to you do I pray.

Prayer is not the soul speaking to itself. Prayer has a recipient, namely, God. Andrew Murray writes, 'Prayer is a true "drawing near" to God, an exercise of inner fellowship with Him.'[2] Many Christians think of prayer as little more than a grim duty, a discipline or exercise that we have to do whether we like it or not. But prayer is our greatest privilege and most potent resource. Prayer is gaining an audience with the Almighty, coming before him personally for worship and fellowship, and setting our petitions before him that are in accordance with his will.

These opening verses describe the various ways we come to God in prayer. David asks God to 'give ear' to his 'words'. That is how we most often pray – thinking or speaking words that are directed to God. But he also asks God to consider his 'groaning', or as some versions have it, his 'sighing'. These are inner desires that we may not be able to articulate clearly. Yet

[1] James Montgomery Boice, *Psalms*, 3 vols. (Grand Rapids: Baker, 1994), vol. 1, p. 44.
[2] Andrew Murray, *The Power of the Blood of Jesus* (Springdale, PA: Whitaker House, 1993), p. 129.

David expects God to receive and interpret them. This is similar to Paul's statement about the way the Spirit helps us in prayer. He writes, 'The Spirit helps us in our weakness. For we do not know what to pray for as we ought, but the Spirit himself intercedes for us with groanings too deep for words' (*Rom.* 8:26). Third, David says, 'Listen to my cry for help' (verse 2, NIV). In danger, fear, or temptation very often the child of God can only cry out to the Father for help. This is an aspect of real prayer, and David asks God to hear him when he cries out. These are the ways we come to God in prayer: *words, groanings,* and *cries*.

Verse 3 adds some valuable counsel about how we should come to God. First, he says we ought to pray having first prepared ourselves and our thoughts. The New International Version translation renders verse 3, 'In the morning, I lay my requests before you.' The word David uses means to 'arrange carefully'. It was used to describe the priest arranging the sacrifice on the altar for the morning offering of each day. This is why the English Standard Version says, 'In the morning I prepare a sacrifice for you.' But David is talking about prayer; he means that to have an effective prayer life we have to arrange our prayers in the same careful way that the priest arranged the sacrifice on the altar.

This means we should prepare our thoughts before we pray. We should think about God's character – his holiness and goodness, his mercy, his power, his love – and also about the works he has done for our salvation. We should reflect on our specific sins so that we might confess them, and on the specific challenges and trials that confront us so that we may be helped. Charles Spurgeon writes, 'Do we not miss very much of the sweetness and efficacy of prayer by a want of careful meditation before it? . . . We too often rush into the presence of God without forethought or humility.'[3] For this reason, I think it is important

---

[3] C. H. Spurgeon, *A Treasury of David*, 3 vols. (Peabody: Hendrickson, n.d.), vol. 1, p. 46.

to keep a prayer journal, especially to organize our ministry of intercessory prayer on behalf of others. However we do it, the extent to which we prepare shows how much we consider prayer a real encounter with the living God.

Verse 3 also suggests that prayer ought to have its own time in the rhythm of our lives. Psalms 4 and 5 go together. In Psalm 4:8, David writes that prayer gives him the peace to lie down and sleep at night. Psalm 5:3 says, 'O LORD, in the morning you hear my voice.' This is a good model for us. A day centred on God ought to begin and end with prayer. As Spurgeon wrote, 'Prayer should be the key of the day and the lock of the night.'[4]

Prayer requires preparation and it should have a regular place in the pattern of our lives. But most important is the *attitude* we adopt when coming to God in prayer. Verse 3 concludes by saying, 'I watch', which means, 'I wait in expectation.' An expectant attitude is a must in prayer. How many of our prayers go unanswered because they are sent heavenward without expecting God to hear and answer them? We should pray believing that God is both able and willing to help, while eagerly looking for his answer to be given.

George Muller was a man who trusted God to answer prayer. He had two close friends who were not saved, and he prayed for them every day for sixty years. Muller's death finally drew near, but he kept on praying for his friends. One was converted by the last sermon Muller ever preached, and the other came to Christ within a year of Muller's death. His example shows us that expectancy in prayer is the key to perseverance in prayer.

Acts chapter 12 shows us the foolishness of praying without expectancy. The apostle Peter was imprisoned with a threat of death hanging over his head. A group of Christians gathered at the house of John Mark's mother to pray for Peter's release. God answered their prayers – even as they prayed – sending an

[4] Ibid.

angel to set the apostle free. Before long, Peter was knocking on the door where the prayer meeting was still taking place. This knocking must have disrupted the concentration of those praying, so a slave girl was sent to drive the intruder away. Recognizing Peter's voice outside, she cried, 'It is Peter!' Their reply is comical, but also tragically typical of our own lack of faith in God's willingness and power to answer prayer. 'You're out of your mind,' they said. Peter, exasperated, continued knocking at the door. Finally, Acts 12:16 tell us, 'When they opened the door and saw him, they were astonished.' Surely we ought not to be like that in prayer. Let us rather tune our ears to the knocking that signifies God answering our petitions.

David prayed and then watched in expectation for God's answer to be given. What was it, we may wonder, that gave him such confidence? Verse 2 shows us. He prayed, 'Give attention to the sound of my cry, my King and my God.' Through faith, David had entered into a covenant relationship with God. He could address God as his King and his God, knowing that the Lord says to those who trust him, 'I will be your God and you will be my people.'

God offers the same kind of relationship to us through Jesus Christ. When doubting Thomas finally believed, he fell before Jesus and cried, 'My Lord and my God!' (*John* 20:28). If you, like Thomas, have trusted in Christ, then you can come to God with the confidence that he is your King and your God, and that, therefore, he will receive you and listen to your prayers. Is this not what we refer to when we conclude our prayers 'In the name of Jesus Christ'?

We are coming through faith in the Saviour God has provided for us and are thus confident of being heard. Jesus told his disciples, 'Whatever you ask of the Father in my name, he will give it to you' (*John* 16:23). God does not suspend his sovereignty and wisdom when we pray, yet the Bible gives us every reason for confidence when we pray according to the will of God and through faith in Christ.

Adoration: The Chief Matter of Prayer

The first stanza of Psalm 5 is itself a primer on coming to God in prayer. But what David says next is also important. What we find in the second stanza, verses 4–6, is that *the chief matter of prayer is adoration of God*. Here, David praises God for his holiness and hatred of all sin:

> You are not a God who delights in wickedness; evil may not dwell with you. The boastful shall not stand before your eyes; you hate all evildoers. You destroy those who speak lies; The LORD abhors the bloodthirsty and deceitful man.

One of the reasons our prayer lives are often ineffective is that we go straight to our list of wants. Note that Psalm 5 does not make a single request of God until verse 8. More than half of the Psalm is coming to God and worshipping him. Our chief aim in prayer ought to be to glorify God, and that is what happens when God's people praise and adore him in prayer. In my view, if there is one chief benefit our prayer lives can receive from the example of the psalms it is that praise is the primary objective of prayer.

Later in this psalm, David is going to seek God's aid against the wicked, so it is no wonder that his praise centres on God's hatred of sin. We, too, ought to arrange our prayers so as to call to mind those attributes of God most related to our situation. God is praised because he takes no pleasure in evil. 'Evil may not dwell with you', David says. 'The boastful shall not stand before your eye; you hate all evildoers.' This is a truth about God that people are quick to forget. We take sin so lightly, but sin is a matter of grave significance to our holy God. Do we praise God for his holiness, as David did?

Reckoning with Sin

This leads naturally to our third point, that *those who pray must reckon with their own sin*. This is the thrust of verse 7, and lies at the heart of this psalm: 'But I, through the abundance of your steadfast love, will enter your house; I will bow down toward your holy temple in the fear of you.'

Notice how significant that 'but' is! David realizes that everything he has said in praise of God's holiness is true regarding himself. God cannot let the wicked into his presence – and David is wicked. The arrogant cannot stand in God's presence – and that will keep David out, too. God hates those who do wrong, he destroys those who lie, and he abhors the bloodthirsty and deceitful. All these characteristics are, in some measure, true of David, as indeed they are true of us all. Unless there is an answer to the problem of our sin, then God's holiness demands our ruin.

'But', David says, 'I will enter your house.' How? 'Through the abundance of your steadfast love.' This is what grants access to those who would otherwise be rejected by God. 'But I will come through your steadfast love.'

The word translated by the English Standard Version as 'steadfast love' is the Hebrew word *chesed*. *Chesed* is such a rich word that it is often translated with more than one English term. The Authorized Version, along with the New International Version, renders it here as *mercy*. The New American Standard Version has it as *lovingkindness*. *Chesed* is the word that signifies God's covenant faithfulness to his people. David, realizing that he himself is a sinner, appeals not to his own character but to God's. Even though he is not righteous, he knows that God is, and that God will be faithful to the gracious covenant he has established.

It is vital for us to understand that this is what makes prayer 'work'. Not a precise formula of words, not some painful discipline, not long utterances or an elaborate display before God. God's faithful covenant love is what makes prayer effective. Many people work so hard trying to 'get prayer right'. God answers our prayers not because we get prayer right, but because, in his loving mercy, he receives his people when they pray. It is on this that we must build our confidence when we approach God and pray.

Notice that David looked to God's 'holy temple', because that is where God's saving grace for sinners was found in his day. The temple was where the animal sacrifices were offered to make atonement for the guilt of sinners, in accordance with God's provision for his people in the law.

This is what enabled a sinner like David to come to the holy God – God's provision of a sacrifice, dying in the sinner's place. The animal sacrifices of David's time were not, in and of themselves, able to atone for human sin. They pointed forward to the true sacrifice, the true Lamb of God, who would come to wash us from our sins once and for all. Therefore, whereas David came to the tabernacle, we come to the cross of Christ, where God's sinless Son was crucified in our place, the righteous for the unrighteous, to bring us to God.

This is the heart of the gospel, apart from which no one can enter into God's presence either now in prayer or later on the Day of Judgment. The psalm tells us that the first danger from which we must be saved is the danger of God's wrath. Our great problem is that God is holy and we are guilty sinners. In Romans 3:13, the apostle Paul quotes the words of verse 9, in which David complains of his enemies, 'Their throat is an open grave; they use their tongues to deceive.' But Paul applies it to the whole human race, in our enmity toward God. Therefore, unless we come by the way God's mercy has provided – by the precious blood of Christ – we may not come to God at all.

This prompts me to ask, have you come to God through faith in Christ? If you have not, you cannot be received by God. His wrath abides on you because of your sin. If you have already done this, you ought to confess your sins regularly, coming to God in prayer confidently, as David did, by 'the abundance of his steadfast love' in Jesus Christ.

Making Requests of God

It is only now, in verse 8, having come to God and worshipped him, and having confessed his need of God's mercy in Christ, that David brings his petitions to God. Having come to God in faith *we should freely and boldly make requests* of him.

David first asks for guidance: 'Lead me, O LORD, in your righteousness because of my enemies; make your way straight before me' (verse 8). He asks God to guide him because God is righteous, whereas his enemies are not trustworthy. Their motives are destructive. 'Their throat is an open grave; they flatter with their tongue' (verse 9).

It is hard to point out any one time in David's life when this was a problem, partly because it was so frequently true. His counsellors, even his sons, plotted against him. His enemies, like King Saul, spread lies about him. David was at times confused and discouraged. So he turned to God for direction. Christians often want God to give some supernatural sign of guidance, but the Bible tells us simply to obey God's Word and pray for wisdom. 'If any of you lacks wisdom, he should ask God, who gives generously to all without reproach, and it will be given him' (*James* 1:5).

The greater our responsibilities, the more keenly we realize our need for God's guidance and help in discernment. We ought also to pray for others, such as our national leaders, who bear great burdens in decision-making. Important decisions ought to be made in conformity with biblical principles and only after prayer for guidance. Abraham Lincoln once confessed, 'I have been driven many times to my knees by the overwhelming conviction that I had nowhere else to go. My own wisdom and that of those about me seemed insufficient.'[5]

David, faced with active opposition, not only prayed for guidance but asked God to help him against his enemies. 'Make them bear their guilt, O God!' he cried. 'Let them fall by their own counsels; because of the abundance of their transgressions cast them out, for they have rebelled against you' (verse 10). Some people complain that it is unworthy for David to ask God

[5] See Cyril J. Barber: *Nehemiah and the Dynamics of Effective Leadership* (Neptune, NJ: Loizeaux Brothers, 1976), p. 19.

to condemn his enemies. But this is not a matter of petty vengeance. What David wants is for righteousness to be upheld, both for his own sake and for God's honour. Being sinners ourselves, we find it hard to pray for God to be glorified in judgment. But in heaven, as the Book of Revelation shows, our purified hearts will glorify God for his justice that punishes sin as well as for his saving mercy. We ought not to be ashamed or afraid to ask God to oppose evil and condemn it in the end, although we must also pray for the salvation of our enemies and persecutors.

Joy and Peace from Prayer

Our fifth and final point comes from the last stanza (verses 11–12) which tells us that God blesses with joy and peace those who pray to him. It is on this theme that David concludes:

> Let all who take refuge in you rejoice; let them ever sing for joy, and spread your protection over them, that those who love your name may exult in you. For you bless the righteous, O LORD; you cover him with favour as with a shield.

Some people lose interest in prayer because they cannot see how God has responded in the way they wanted. That is foolish for several reasons. It fails to see the value of worship in prayer; it fails to understand that God is wiser than us and that we should be happy to let him work out his own answers to our prayers. But it also fails to realize that prayer changes us; God blesses us with joy and peace.

David sees prayer as a refuge and he knows that those who sail into this harbour are filled with gladness. In its calm waters our hearts are lifted into song. Though our outward circumstances are filled with danger and turmoil, God speaks peace to our hearts, just as Jesus once stilled the waves and calmed the storm. Paul speaks of a similar blessing that comes to us in prayer, in a passage that ought to be familiar to every Christian:

Do not be anxious about anything, but in everything by prayer and supplication with thanksgiving let your requests be made known to God. And the peace of God, which surpasses all understanding, will guard your hearts and your minds in Christ Jesus (*Phil.* 4:6–7).

In the last two verses of Psalm 5, David uses two metaphors to describe how this happens. First, he asks, 'Spread your protection over them.' This recalls the way a mother hen spreads her wings over the heads of her chicks so they can no longer see the source of their fear, but only her calming presence. So it is for those who see God in his might, spreading forth his protecting wings. 'If God is for us,' the Scripture asks, 'who can be against us?' (*Rom.* 8:31). Under his wings, God's people are filled with joy and peace.

David adds, as he concludes in verse 12, 'For you bless the righteous, O Lord; you cover him with favour as with a shield.' In ancient warfare, shields were tall and wide, covering the entire body so that no weapon could penetrate and do harm. David says this is what God does for the righteous, that is, those who look to him in faith and are justified through Jesus Christ. God's people are surrounded by his unfailing love as a shield. Nothing can reach us except what he permits as being ultimately for our good. This is how he comforts us in prayer, spreading forth his wings, reaching out his arms as a shield, giving peace to our souls and calm to our hearts.

In the early days of the Protestant Reformation, Martin Luther was summoned to Augsburg to appear before the Roman Catholic authorities who demanded that he recant his heretical teachings. Since others convicted of heresy had been burned at the stake, Luther had reason to fear for his life. Many of his friends urged him not to go, but Luther's prince, the Elector of Saxony, guaranteed him safe passage. Luther went forth, resolved to stand upon God's Word, even though the emperor, the pope, and the examining cardinal were united against him. When he arrived, one of the cardinal's officials mocked Luther, asking where he could hope to find shelter, with all the world against him, if his patron, the Elector of Saxony, should desert him? Luther replied that he would be safe, 'Under the shield of heaven.' History records that Luther was not forced to recant nor was he killed, but went on to bless the world with the gospel he had recovered. As Psalm 5 says, God blesses the righteous, surrounding them with favour as with a shield.

Can you say this is true for you? If not, do what David did and what Martin Luther did; confess your guilt and sin to God, casting yourself on his mercy in Jesus Christ. If you have done that, then you ought to be eager to pray to him, approaching him in worship, presenting your requests and concerns, and receiving from your Lord the joy and the peace he supplies to his believing people.

8

FROM FEAR TO FAITH
PSALM 56

When I am afraid, I put my trust in you. In God, whose word I praise, in God I trust; I shall not be afraid. What can flesh do to me? (*Psa.* 56:3–4).

'What can man do to me?' That is the question posed by Psalm 56. According to the things we read and hear in the news, the answer is that man can do quite a lot. Today's news regularly includes reports of the devastation caused by suicide bombers, business executives who lie to investors about the value of their companies, people who kill, rape, and abuse others. What can man do to me? Man can kill you, betray your trust, steal your money, destroy your dreams and ambitions, and tear your heart in pieces. Knowing this, the writer of Psalm 56 frankly tells us he is afraid. Very often we are too.

The author of this psalm is Israel's King David, one of the great men of the Bible. It was written at a time when he was vulnerable and weak, when he was viciously opposed by men who hated him. That is why he was afraid. But in this psalm he combats his fear with faith, and he teaches us to do the same. There are two voices calling back and forth, contending with each other in the heart. First, there is *the voice of fear*: we hear it in verses 1 and 2, then again in verses 5 and 6. Countering this is *the voice of faith* that makes up the great refrain of this psalm: 'When I am afraid, I put my trust in you . . . What can flesh do to me?' (verses 3–4).

We have been considering the subject of communion with God as we have studied a number of psalms. Having begun by describing the *relationship* that believers have with the Lord, we are now considering the *consequences* of a life lived in fellowship with God. This reminds us that there is such a thing as the Christian life. There is a life that is enjoyed by those who are in Christ and who walk with God. It is manifested not so much on the outside but on the inside – in our character, our attitude, our demeanour, our strength in the face of life's tumults and tempests.

Psalm 56 leads our exploration in this direction. Here we consider the man of God as he faces fear with faith. Here is a believer who responds to the terror of real opposition, and hatred, and danger, and finds from God a courage that leads to godly thanksgiving and determination to obey.

The Voice of Fear

First, let us hear the voice of fear with which the psalm begins in verses 1 and 2: 'Be gracious to me, O God, for man tramples on me; all day long an attacker oppresses me; my enemies trample on me all day long, for many attack me proudly.'

David prays for help here because of the fury of his attackers. He is hotly pursued. Verses 5 and 6 tell us the nature of the attack: 'All day long they injure my cause; all their thoughts are against me for evil. They stir up strife, they lurk; they watch my steps, as they have waited for my life.' David's enemies want to ruin his reputation; but more than that, they want to bring an end to his very life.

According to the inscription that precedes this psalm, Psalm 56 was composed at one of the low points of David's life, 'when the Philistines seized him in Gath'. After David killed the giant Goliath, his fame and prestige rose meteorically. This caused King Saul to envy him as a potential rival and, ultimately, to hate David. In fact, David was completely loyal, but Saul's animosity forced the young hero to flee. 1 Samuel chapters 20–22 tell of his desperate flight. First, he sought aid from the priests at Nob. They gave him bread and the sword of Goliath. The priests, however, were not able to protect David; in fact, when Saul learned of their help to David, he ruthlessly put them all to death. Desperate and panicked, David fled from Israel. He decided to enter Philistia, home to Israel's chief enemies, perhaps thinking they would welcome a fugitive from King Saul.

When David arrived at Gath he realized he had made a terrible mistake. Gath was, after all, Goliath's hometown. Imagine the townspeople setting their eyes on the man who had so remarkably slain their great champion. Adding insult to injury, he now had the audacity to come bearing the very sword of the slain hometown hero! Far from embracing David, who now realized he must have been crazy to come here, they ran to their king, Achish, crying, 'Is not this David the king of the land? Did they not sing to one another of him in dances, "Saul has struck down his thousands, and David his ten thousands"?' (*1 Sam.* 21:11). That is, tens of thousands of Philistines!

The account tells us that David was 'much afraid'. We can see him as they laid hands on him. 'I must have been crazy . . . I must have been crazy . . .', and in that way he devised his plan. 'I will act as if I am crazy.' And that is what he did: 'So he . . . pretended to be insane . . . and made marks on the doors of the gate and let his spittle run down his beard' (*1 Sam.* 21:13). The superstitious Philistines had a belief that anyone who killed or even held a madman would be cursed, so David's ruse succeeded in saving his life, if not his dignity.

What an embarrassing episode for David! The account reminds us how honest the Bible is, telling us the truth about the sin and folly of its heroes. This also dramatizes what tends to happen when we take matters into our own hands, saving ourselves through worldly means rather than trusting in God. Our plan may work and we may wriggle to a position of safety, but we may degrade ourselves in the process. It is noteworthy that the Bible shows no record of David praying during the whole episode of his flight from Nob to Gath; no wonder that he fell into such error. But his folly seems to have jarred him to his senses; having experienced the futility of his own strategies, he was ready to turn again to the Lord, which is what we find in Psalm 56. David had let go of God and fallen into folly, but God had not let go of him. Having escaped from danger, David now turns back to the Lord in prayer.

The note of thanksgiving found in this psalm leads us to think that David wrote it, not during, but after his captivity in Gath. However, he was still desperate, with no choice but to return to the land of King Saul, who still wanted to kill him. And so the voice of fear rises from his heart. This time fear did not lead him to foolish and desperate acts or self-reliant strategies. Having remembered God, fear led David to turn to him in faith. 'When I am afraid,' he prays, 'I put my trust in you' (verse 3).

How often this is the case with us too; it takes fear and failure to spur us on to faith. God places us in situations we do not want to be in where we are frightened and unsettled. He does it to provoke this response of faith. Peter says in his first epistle that trials come 'so that your faith – of greater worth than gold, which perishes even though refined by fire – may be proved genuine and may result in praise, glory, and honour when Jesus Christ is revealed' (*1 Pet.* 1:7, NIV). The response God desires from us is the one David exhibits here: 'When I am afraid, I put my trust in you.'

The Voice of Faith

David's recovered faith provides the chorus of this psalm, occurring in verse 4, and then in slightly altered form in verses 10–11: 'In God, whose word I praise, in the LORD whose word

I praise, in God I trust; I shall not be afraid. What can man do to me?'

Here we see that the key ingredient of faith is *trust*. Saving faith is not merely assenting to statements of truth or to the idea of God. It is trust. To trust is to rely on someone; in this case to rely on God for salvation. When we trust we are ready to act with confidence; having an object of trust provides a defence against fear. David's faith sees God and finds in him a source of protection, help, and blessing. Therefore he is afraid no longer.

I can imagine David writing this psalm, not only with a pen in his hand but with a sword across his knees – the sword of Goliath. I can see him gazing on that mighty weapon as he wrote: 'In God I trust; I shall not be afraid. What can flesh do to me?' It would have reminded him of his greatest triumph. Goliath was an incredibly large giant whose size and strength terrified the whole of Saul's army. Trusting in God, David defeated him with a slingshot; Goliath could not harm him. 'You come to me with a sword and with a spear and with a javelin,' David had cried to the giant of Gath, 'but I come to you in the name of the LORD of hosts, the God of the armies of Israel, whom you have defied. This day, the LORD will deliver you into my hand, and I will strike you down and cut off your head . . . For the battle is the LORD's, and he will give you into our hand' (*1 Sam.* 17:45–47).

David had trusted God in the past. When he looked out on to the battlefield he saw not only the Philistine giant, but also the giant God who towered high above the big Philistine warrior. It is this he recalls now after having acted in unbelief and fear. He has come to his senses and exercises the faith with which he had conquered before: 'In God I trust; I shall not be afraid. What can flesh do to me?'

What a difference exists between faith of this kind and mere fleshly bravado. This was trust in God, faith resting in who God is, in his might, faithfulness and love.

J. B. Phillips spoke of this in a little book entitled *Your God Is Too Small*. 'The trouble with many people today', he begins, 'is that they have not found a God big enough for modern needs.'[1] The book describes the way religious people have cultivated little views of God. They think of God as a nagging conscience, or a grand but indifferent old man, or a distant cosmic overseer too busy to worry about us, or a meek and mild Jesus who looks on with a vague and distant affection – more a statue than God – or again, as a sort of spiritual Santa Claus to whom we send our list of wishes. These are little views of God, man-made views of God. How far they are from the God of the Bible, who is sovereign, almighty, omnipresent, all-knowing, perfect in holiness, power, and love. God says in the Bible, 'I am the LORD your God, the Holy One of Israel, your Saviour' (*Isa.* 43:3).

David knew and trusted a God who towers above the world and who cares for his people. If I trust in God, he reasoned, what can flesh, the power of man, however great, do to me? Isaiah said, 'All flesh is grass, and all its beauty is like the flower of the field . . . The grass withers, the flower fades, but the word of our God will stand for ever' (*Isa.* 40:6–8).

This is why we need to study and reflect upon the attributes of God – who and what God really is. When we learn of God's goodness, holiness, love, his omnipotent power and wisdom, his complete sovereignty over all things, our confidence in him grows. Our faith, like David's, can only be as strong as its object; when we know God and see all our foes in comparison to him, we find that our faith can conquer all fear.

First, David trusts God. But, second, we see here that his faith is grounded in God's Word. He says, 'In God, whose word I praise . . . in God I trust.'

What do we mean by God's Word? In David's case this would include statements God made to him personally. In 1 Samuel 16, God sent the prophet Samuel to anoint David as Israel's king; God had promised that David would one day sit upon the

[1] J. B. Phillips, *Your God Is Too Small* (New York, Collier, 1961), p. 7.

throne. David remembered this and trusted what God had said. But more importantly, when we speak of God's Word we mean his written revelation – the Bible. Surely this was in David's mind as well. In his day, the Bible consisted of the Pentateuch, the first five books of the Bible. This was God's Word and it revealed God's mighty saving works in the Exodus. Israel's back was to the Red Sea, with Pharaoh's army bearing down on them. But Moses commanded the people to trust the Lord, and the Lord rescued them through the parted waters of the Red Sea. This and other passages in his Bible confirmed to David that the Lord answers those who call on him. He saves those who trust in him. It is noteworthy that when David made his own contributions to the Bible, in the Psalms, this was something he strongly emphasized. Summing up all he had learned by experience and in Scripture, David praised the Lord in Psalm 22:4, writing, 'In you our fathers trusted; they trusted, and you delivered them.'

This is how we find courage to trust in God, through the sure and certain testimony of his Word. This is what a Christian is, someone who believes God's Word and on its authority trusts God to be his Saviour. It is especially in the Bible's promises that we find the confidence to trust in God. J. C. Ryle asserts:

> There are 'shalls' and 'wills' in God's treasury for every condition. About God's infinite mercy and compassion; about His readiness to receive all who repent and believe; about His willingness to forgive, pardon and absolve the chief of sinners; about His power to change hearts and alter our corrupt nature; about the encouragements to pray and hear the gospel and draw near to the throne of grace; about strength for duty, comfort in trouble, guidance in perplexity, help in sickness, consolation in death, support under bereavement, happiness beyond the grave, reward in glory – about all these things there is an abundant supply of promises in the Word.[2]

[2] J. C. Ryle, *Holiness* (1877; repr. Durham: Evangelical Press, 1979), pp. 261–3.

The Christian also trusts in God and the Word he has spoken particularly as they find their focus in the Person and work of Jesus Christ. The Gospels are filled with Jesus' many 'I will' statements. He promises rest to the weary soul: 'Come to me, all who labour and are heavy laden, and I will give you rest' (*Matt.* 11:28). He gives us confidence for eternal life, through faith in him, saying it is the Father's will that 'everyone who looks on the Son and believes in him should have eternal life, and I will raise him up on the last day' (*John* 6:40). It is because of Jesus' promises in God's Word that we know that all will be well for those who trust in him: 'I will not leave you as orphans; I will come to you . . . Because I live, you also will live' (*John* 14:18–19). Such promises have given hope to vast numbers of God's people, as well as joy in the face of death and persecution. We can have the same in the lesser trials and dangers we face.

In fact, two of the greatest statements that the New Testament makes about Christ draw on verses in this psalm. Verse 13, the last verse, thanks God because 'You have delivered my soul from death, yes, my feet from falling, that I may walk before God in the light of life.' It is possible that Jesus had this verse explicitly in mind when he said 'I am the light of the world. Whoever follows me will not walk in darkness, but will have the light of life' (*John* 8:12). When we look to Jesus in trusting faith, he promises to light our path in the way of eternal life, just as David, for all his danger, was confident of finding a way to safety. Also, the writer of Hebrews picks up on David's assertion from verses 4 and 11: '[God] has said, "I will never leave you nor forsake you." So we can confidently say, "The Lord is my helper; I will not fear; what can man do to me?"' (*Heb.* 13: 5–6).

Here is the Christian claim, the faith that sustained David even in his time of fear. Jesus Christ invites all to trust in him and receive a full, complete and secure salvation. He calls to sinners and offers forgiveness; to the weak he offers strength, to the blind he gives sight, to the spiritually dead he imparts eternal life. He tells his people that, whatever the world may do to our bodies, God will preserve our souls. We can be afflicted for a little while in this world. Our bodies can be made to suffer. Our hearts may be broken. But the wounds inflicted by mortal man cannot touch the eternal treasures stored up for us in Christ. Indeed, for the Christian, all things are made to work for our good – even sorrows, which draw us nearer to Christ. That is how Paul reasoned: 'If God is for us,' he asked, 'who can be against us?' (*Rom.* 8:31). Jesus shed his blood to save us from sin and from the world; safe in his hands we can say with David, 'In God I trust; I will not be afraid. What can flesh do to me?'

When God Is Big

Psalm 56 shows us that when faith meets fear with a God who is big enough to save us, the believer receives courage to live for God. This is the very thing we need if we are to honour God and make our lives count for his kingdom.

Christian counsellor Edward Welch has written an excellent book entitled, *When People Are Big and God Is Small.* This is the way most of us live, he argues, fearing man instead of God. He lists the things people are afraid of, things like humiliation, rejection, emotional or physical harm. The thing you fear, he says, will always control you. So our behaviour is dictated by what other people do or think or say. Our attitudes are shaped by how we think people perceive us. What determines our peace and joy is how others treat us. This goes on all through life; teenagers give in to 'peer pressure', adults become 'people pleasers'. If it gets bad enough we label them as 'co-dependent'. No doubt many of us are like this; indeed, all of us are guilty of this to some extent. In every case the real problem is a fear of man instead of the fear of God. Welch writes, 'The first task in escaping the snare of the fear of man is to know that *God* is awesome and glorious, not other people.'[3]

[3] Edward T. Welch, *When People Are Big and God Is Small* (Phillipsburg, NJ: P & R, 1997), p. 95.

Martin Luther was a man who feared the Lord. In other words he comprehended God's holiness and greatness, the gravity that attends God's ways and commands, and the seriousness of God's judgment. Compared to these, the things of this world paled into insignificance. Fearful about the future well-being of his soul during a violent thunderstorm, Luther decided to became a monk and entered the monastery, seeking salvation by becoming a religious man. The fear of God kept him from being dissuaded by his father, who ridiculed this decision. As he progressed, Luther gradually lost faith in the Roman Catholic system of works-righteousness. Why? Because he feared the Lord. In his soul he knew that he was a guilty sinner and that God is a holy, great, and terrible God. No amount of sincerely performed good works could ever placate a holy and truly righteous God, and neither could the religious rituals he had also tried to depend on.

In terror for his soul, Luther searched the Bible and there discovered the gospel of salvation through faith alone in Christ alone. His fears were turned to faith when he saw that God had provided a great salvation through the atoning death of his Son. Finding salvation through faith alone in Christ alone by grace alone, here Luther took his stand.

It is no surprise, then, that once Luther found God's way of salvation, nothing could move him from his place of safety. His first books against Roman Catholicism caused Luther to be summoned before the Diet of Worms in 1521. The threat of death by burning was real. His accuser demanded he recant of his teachings, but Luther replied, 'I must walk in fear of the Lord.' He concluded with these immortal words, 'My conscience is captive to the Word of God. I cannot and will not recant anything . . . God help me. Here I stand, I cannot do otherwise. Amen.'[4]

---

[4] Roland Bainton, *Here I Stand: A Life of Martin Luther* (New York: New American Library, 1950), pp. 143–4.

That is the courageous faith we need today. It is a faith we will find only in the place Luther found it, and where David found it too, the Word of God. It counts just as much in the little affairs of our lives as in the great deeds of men like Martin Luther. When you don't give in to the sexual allures of a perverted society; when you proclaim Christ in the face of ridicule; when you refuse to cheat, lie, slander, or hate; when you derive your standards and pursue your goals, not in accordance with a godless culture's rules, but according to God's living Word; then God is praised in heaven and on earth. Facing fears that were as real as any you may face, David said, 'In God I trust; I shall not be afraid. What can man do to me?' If Christians are going to walk with integrity before God and make a difference in their generation, it will be with the courage that comes from faith of this kind.

Faith Conquering Fear

I will conclude this chapter with a few observations. The first is that trust is something we have to learn to exercise throughout the whole course of our lives. David starts with the voice of fear. Faith rallies in verse 3, but by verse 5 fear has the upper hand again, before giving way a second time to faith in verse 10. That is how our lives often go, fear and faith struggling together. This period in David's life, as he fled from an undeserved hostility, moving from one danger to the next, tested and increased David's faith until it was stronger than before. The psalm that follows, Psalm 57, was written during the very next phase of his fugitive career and it rises to an even loftier height. Its chorus sings, 'Be exalted, O God, above the heavens! Let your glory be over all the earth!' (verse 5, 11). The goal of our lives, is to grow strong in faith, and thus to escape our fears, and to glorify the Lord.

Second, our growth in faith is strengthened through communion with God in prayer. Verses 8 and 9 show how important prayer was to the recovery of David's faith. He cries,

'You have kept count of my tossings; put my tears in your bottle. Are they not in your book? Then my enemies will turn back in the day when I call. This I know, that God is for me.' David asks God not merely to record his tears, but to capture them, to treasure them in a bottle. He cries upon God's shoulder; though he feels so alone he knows that God cares about him. It is while resting his troubled head on God's shoulder that he feels the strength of God's arm, and senses the care in God's heart. In this way prayer restores vitality to his faith. The challenge of our lives is to grow in faith, and in this quest we cannot succeed if we neglect prayer.

My third observation comes from verse 12, which says, 'I must perform my vows to you, O God; I will render thank offerings to you.' This reveals what happens when faith overcomes fear. David is delivered from despair and now thinks about thanksgiving and worship. He looks forward to the day when he can return to the tabernacle and present his thank offerings to the Lord. One of the marks of an active faith is humble thanksgiving that longs to praise the Lord. Indeed, the surest sign that we are trusting God, especially in our trials, is that we have gratitude for him in our heart and that we praise him for his faithful love.

Finally, the psalm concludes with the resolve that comes to those who trust the Lord. Franklin Roosevelt famously said, 'The only thing we have to fear is fear itself.'[5] That may or may not have been true of America when Roosevelt said it, but it is certainly true of those who trust in God. We leave the circumstances and dangers to his care, overcoming our fear through faith in him, and we determine to serve him in all things. That is what David did. He resolves in verse 13 to 'walk before God in the light of life'.

Have you determined to do that? Silence your fear with the voice of faith. Trust in God; trust in his Word; trust the Saviour who died and rose again and reigns forever, mighty to save – our Lord Jesus Christ. This psalm is preceded by one of the

[5] First Inaugural Address, 1933.

lowest episodes in David's life, but it is followed by one of his greatest periods of godliness. The same can be true of you, no matter how you may have stumbled or fallen in unbelief, if now you will trust the Lord.

Jesus said, 'I am the light of the world. Whoever follows me will not walk in darkness, but will have the light of life' (*John* 8:12). He was talking about the life of godliness, obedience, spiritual purpose, power, peace, and joy. Look to Christ in faith – for the first time or once again; be cleansed by his blood and renewed by his Spirit. Embolden yourself in the promises of God's Word and through prayer. Then, fortified by that faith, determine that you will follow Jesus Christ. Then you will find, as David found, light for darkness, faith for fear, and courage to live to the glory of God.

9

PATHWAY TO JOY
PSALM 16

The lines have fallen for me in pleasant places; indeed, I have a beautiful inheritance . . . You make known to me the path of life; in your presence there is fullness of joy; at your right hand are pleasures for evermore (*Psa.* 16:6, 11).

O ne of the clearest signs of communion with God is the experience of joy in all circumstances. When we say that we want to grow in our relationship with God, one of the things we imply is that we want to have the Lord's own joy at all times. The famous opening question of the *Westminster Shorter Catechism* reminds us that joy is an integral part of God's purpose for mankind: 'What is the chief end of man?' 'Man's chief end is to glorify God, and to *enjoy* him forever.' The apostle Paul concurs, listing joy as one of the great characteristics of life in the kingdom: 'The kingdom of God is not a matter of eating and drinking but of righteousness and peace and joy in the Holy Spirit' (*Rom.* 14:17).

In our study of Psalm 1, I pointed out that everyone wants to be happy. The same thing could be said about joy. But joy, as the Bible speaks of it, is quite different from what most people think of as happiness. When people speak of happiness, they tend to mean 'having a good time'. They are talking about having pleasing experiences and avoiding those that are unpleasant. The emphasis is on circumstances, which determine whether or not they are happy.

Despite what many people may think, Christians are not against having a good time. But the Bible focuses our attention on a higher, greater, and more durable joy that springs from the presence of the indwelling Holy Spirit. This spiritual joy does not depend on favourable outward circumstances; it is a gift of God's grace and can be experienced in any and every circumstance.

The Bible commands us to pursue this joy. Paul writes: 'Rejoice in the Lord always; again I will say Rejoice' (*Phil.* 4:4). Yet the cry of many Christians is, 'Would that I had such joy!' For all who feel this way, Psalm 16 leads us along 'the pathway to joy' and brings before us spiritual steps that lead to God and to the joy that comes from him.

Psalm 16: A Psalm of Joy

The author of this psalm is King David, and he wrote it, like so many others, in a time of personal difficulty. The psalm divides neatly into four portions. First is *a prayer for help*.

Verse 1 reads, 'Preserve me, O God, for in you I take refuge.' We do not know the exact circumstances that gave rise to this plea, but we can see that David was in some kind of danger. It is possible that the psalm comes from the period in his life when David was a fugitive from King Saul. David had become a national hero by slaying the giant Goliath. Saul rewarded David, but secretly envied him. Before long Saul's malice ripened, and on two occasions he made attempts on David's life, forcing the young hero to flee. For a period of some years David became an outlaw fugitive, though innocent of any wrong-doing. He lived on the run, in fear and in poverty, without a place to lay his head. We can understand, then, why so many of his psalms begin like this one does: 'Preserve me, O God, for in you I take refuge.'

The threats David faced are not uncommon in our world. People are often the victims of the envy, greed, and malice of others. Life in this fallen world involves familiarity with sorrow, disease, and ultimately death. Therefore, if we are to know abiding joy on this side of heaven, it will have to be in such a world as this. In other words, the context in which godly joy arises is that of hardship, difficulty, emotional pain, and sorrow. Jesus told his disciples: 'In the world you will have tribulation. But take heart; I have overcome the world' (*John* 16:33).

If Christians know joy only when things are going well, we cannot claim to be different from anybody else, nor can we claim that Christianity possesses any special power. If that is so, there is no compelling reason why people should become Christians. The world knows how to have joy when all is well; the tragedy is that its joy is fleeting and utterly fails when troubles come. Our joy, therefore, must be different. C. H. Spurgeon wrote:

> Any fool can sing in the day. When the cup is full, man draws inspiration from it. When wealth rolls in abundance round about him, any man can sing to the praise of a God who gives a plenteous harvest . . . [but] songs in the night come only from God; they are not in the power of men.[1]

It is to God's glory that Christians know a joy that is independent of circumstances, 'songs in the night' that come only from God. David seems to have known this, because here in verse 1 he begins by taking his troubles to the Lord. He might have focused on the circumstances themselves, but he would have found no power there; he might have dwelt on the thoughts or actions of others, but that would not have quietened his heart. Instead, and wisely, he fixed his eyes on the Lord: 'Preserve me, O God,' he cried, 'for in you I take refuge.' As David brings his plea to God and turns his thoughts to the Lord, he has, in fact, taken his first step in the path of an all-conquering joy.

[1] *Spurgeon's Sermons* (Grand Rapids: Baker, 1983), vol. 2, pp. 169–70.

David's Application of Faith

In verses 2–8 we see David's *actions* in the light of this prayer. He has reached out to God for safety and strength. From that refuge, he now turns back to his situation in verses 2–4, taking a sort of spiritual inventory of his circumstances. In verse 1 he turned to God. Having done so, he now very deliberately applies his faith, his God-centred perspective, to every factor in the equation around him. This is how he gains his spiritual equilibrium. Very thoroughly, he reconsiders everything in the light of his knowledge of God.

In verse 2, David acknowledges God's saving presence in his affairs: 'I say to the LORD, "You are my Lord; I have no good apart from you."' He uses two names for God, both of which read 'Lord' in our English Bibles. First, he describes God as 'Yahweh', which our Bibles show as LORD in small capital letters. This is the covenant name of God, the personal name he gave to Israel. It is the name that binds God to his people, and in this way David reminds himself of God's covenant faithfulness to him: 'I say to Yahweh'.

David then addresses God by using the Hebrew word *adonai*, which means *Master* or *Lord*. 'You are my Lord,' he says. David is like a weak vassal who sees the enemy approaching, but who looks up and sees the castle of his Lord, and then the Lord himself arrayed for battle. This gives him courage and, in return, he acknowledges his full dependence on the Lord. In particular, it is God's sovereignty and goodness he has in view here: 'You are my Lord; I have no good apart from you' (verse 2).

Next he turns his eye upon fellow believers, saying in verse 3: 'As for the saints in the land, they are the excellent ones, in whom is all my delight.' David sees fellow believers, those who also look to the Lord for salvation, and he is encouraged by his solidarity with them. How uplifting it is to realize that we are part of the people of God and that we love them! Do you look around you and find that you love other Christians, that you long for their blessing, that you ache when they suffer? Let that serve as a strong testimony to you that God has made you his own, a genuine member of his flock. 'We know that we have passed out of death into life,' the Apostle John informs us, 'because we love the brothers' (*1 John* 3:14).

Thirdly, in verse 4, he turns his gaze upon the unbelieving and idolatrous world around him: 'The sorrows of those who run after another god shall multiply; their drink offerings of blood I will not pour out or take their names on my lips.' In this way he gains a believing perspective on those people who seem to have it so good apart from God, realizing that in the end theirs is not a position he should envy. He vows not to pursue their way of life.

One of the most damaging things for a Christian is to envy the prosperity and power of the unbelieving world. David realizes that the wicked will not prosper in the end; in the end God will judge the world and vindicate his people. By applying his faith, David remembers this, and that keeps him from despair.

My Portion and My Cup

In verses 5 to 8 we see the new and godly *attitude* that results from David applying his faith to his situation. Look at the difference this has made! In verse 1, David was frightened, anxious, perhaps even panicked; now, after a brief re-evaluation through the application of his faith, he says these great lines:

> The LORD is my chosen portion and my cup; you hold my lot. The lines have fallen for me in pleasant places; indeed, I have a beautiful inheritance (verses 5–6).

What a remarkable change of perspective! By considering his circumstances through faith, David calms his heart in submission to God. He accepts his portion cheerfully because he has seen God, and he remembers God's sovereignty and goodness. 'You are my Lord; I have no good apart from you' (verse 2). You are 'my chosen portion and my cup . . . The lines have fallen for me in pleasant places' (verses 5–6).

Few things are more difficult for us than to peacefully submit to the circumstances God has allotted us. David has taken the things he knows to be true about God and he has also seen himself for what he is – a true member of God's people – and then he calls to mind the tragic end that awaits the ungodly. With these truths, he quietens his heart and submits to God's will. This is a product of communion with God through a life of prayer that feeds upon the instruction of God's Word. We calmly rely on God's sovereignty and goodness and are enabled to submit to his wise and loving provision which is revealed in our circumstances. We come to know God, and knowing him, to trust him with joy.

This is what caused the Apostle Paul to write, 'We know that for those who love God all things work together for good, for those who are called according to his purpose' (*Rom.* 8:28). Not all things are good, but we know that, in his sovereignty, God uses them for good. So in the midst of our trials we can say of the day to come: 'Surely I have a good inheritance.' This is why Paul tells us not merely to pray, but to offer our petitions with thanksgiving. For then, 'the peace of God, which surpasses all understanding, will guard your hearts and your minds in Christ Jesus' (*Phil.* 4:7). Is this not the experience of David in this Psalm?

Therefore My Heart Is Glad

We know that David has truly submitted to the Lord in his heart, because he goes on to *praise* him. His song of praise is recorded in verses 7–8:

> I bless the LORD who gives me counsel; in the night also my heart instructs me. I have set the LORD always before me; because he is at my right hand, I shall not be shaken.

David is now close to receiving joy; we know this because we find him praising God. Worship takes the submissive heart and leads it into joy. A cold, resentful submission will never produce joy, but the Christian who bends the knee in thankful worship will rise with gladness in his heart. The reason for this is that we were created to worship God, and worshipping him is what is best for us. Joy comes to us when we are acting in accordance with the divine design for our lives, as we fulfil our highest purpose through worship. Worship means praising God and we can do it anywhere, anytime, and in all circumstances. As we worship with glad and sincere hearts, we feel God's pleasure and receive joy from the Lord. This is the key to joy. Psalm 71:23 shows us the link between worship and joy: 'My lips will shout for joy, when I sing praises to you.'

So let me ask you a vital question: Can you worship God in the valley of sorrow and in the shadow of death, in the presence of difficulty, trial, and pain? Are you walking on this pathway to joy? It begins with faith, which leads to a submissive attitude towards God's provision, and in turn, lifts up our hearts in praise. Or is your worship essentially mercenary, a product of circumstance rather than a sincere response to the knowledge and worthiness of God? Such worship does not come automatically, nor is it easy. This is not a trick or gimmick. Instead, joy in the midst of trials is a by-product of a faith that submits to God's will because it knows he is sovereign and good. And how important this is! It will determine the kind of life we will live in this world of sorrow. Will we worship the Giver himself because he is worthy of our worship – both in times of plenty and in want – or will we merely worship him because of the gifts he gives?

Job was a man who praised God when things were going well in his life. But the devil insisted that Job's praise was merely based on his material prosperity. The Lord therefore allowed Satan to afflict Job in order to test the sincerity of his faith. When Job began to suffer, his friends wrongly concluded that there must have been some secret wickedness in his life that was the cause of this punishment. But here we have an example of what is often true, that in a sin-cursed world like ours, suffering and trial will sometimes have little or nothing to do with our own sin and failure.

Job's friends accused him; his wife looked on her husband, covered as he was with boils, and said in effect, 'Why don't you just curse God and die!' (*Job* 2:9). Do you ever feel like that? But the key to Job's life was that he did not curse God. He submitted to God's will as revealed in his life. He said, 'Shall we receive good from God, and shall we not receive evil?' (*Job* 2:10). Job praised God in the midst of his misery: 'The LORD gave, and the LORD has taken away; blessed be the name of the LORD' (*Job* 1:21). In life and in death he committed himself to God's sovereign, gracious will: 'Though he slay me, I will hope in him' (*Job* 13:15). That is real worship, arising from Job's faith in God – a faith that was not misplaced. In the end, God vindicated Job and blessed him even more than before.

Anyone can praise God in plenty and comfort. But to be able to worship God at the sickbed of a child, at the graveside of a husband, in the tumult of war, or amidst the sorrows of a broken world causes the angels to gaze on in silence, shuts the mouths of demons, and makes the watching world stand up and take notice.

A couple of years ago, a car carrying a minister and his family was involved in a head-on collision. The wife woke from her coma to learn that her husband and one of her children had died in the accident. Their little boy had just unbuckled his seatbelt to pick up a crayon when the crash happened. Do you know what the woman said when she learned of her great loss? With tears streaming down her face she said, 'God is good in all he does.' That wasn't trite. It was glorious. Seraphim, with burning eyes, saw the glory of God in the heart of that sorrowful believer.

That is what the apostle meant when he wrote, 'This is the victory that has overcome the world – our faith' (*1 John* 5:4). We are kept in this world to demonstrate such faith to the glory of God. When we do so, the result is joy. As we worship God in the midst of our tribulations, the Holy Spirit sends into our hearts a joy that is born of heaven. This joy is independent of the circumstances of this world. This is why I said that spiritual joy is the best indicator of real communion with God. Verse 11 says, 'In your presence there is fullness of joy', and that is as high an expression of communion with God as any in all of Scripture.

David worshipped God. He set the Lord before him and was not shaken. He praised God for giving him counsel. Isn't that interesting? He doesn't say that God removed the danger; he doesn't say that God changed his circumstances. But God changed *him*. He counselled David in the way of faith and instructed his heart. David's grasp was so tenuous and weak, but when he reached out to God, he found a strong support. He said, 'I shall not be shaken' (verse 8).

'Therefore', he goes on to say, 'my heart is glad, and my whole being rejoices.' You see the relationship: 'I will praise the Lord . . . therefore my heart is glad.' That is the secret, if you want to call it that, of abiding joy in this world. God wants us to give him our hearts so that he might become our strength and that our joy might be found in him.

The Indirectness of the Christian Life

Let me take a moment to probe one key insight here, and that is *the indirectness of the Christian life*. Everybody wants happiness, and yet so few seem to find it. The reason is that they are seeking for happiness in the wrong way. I quoted the *Westminster Shorter Catechism*, which teaches us that we were created to glorify God and enjoy him forever. We are to worship *him*, not happiness; we are to find our joy *in the Lord* and not in things or circumstances.

When Martyn Lloyd-Jones was preaching on one of Jesus' beatitudes – 'Blessed are they that hunger and thirst after righteousness' – he observed:

> We are not to hunger and thirst after blessedness; we are not to hunger and thirst after happiness. But that is what most people

are doing . . . Whenever you put happiness before righteousness, you will be doomed to misery. That is the great message of the Bible from beginning to end. They alone are truly happy who are seeking to be righteous.[2]

This is what I mean by the *indirectness* of the Christian life, the *indirect* route to joy. 'Seek first the kingdom of God and his righteousness,' Jesus taught, 'and all these things will be added to you' (*Matt.* 6:33). We are not to twist our lives around seeking personal fulfilment; rather we are to give ourselves to the worship of God at all times, to doing his will, and to trusting him alone. When we live our lives for him we discover, almost to our surprise, that joy has been growing in our hearts along the way. Jesus said, 'Whoever would save his life will lose it, but whoever loses his life for my sake will find it' (*Matt.* 16:25).

Resurrection Joy

The Lord Jesus Christ is the supreme example of the principles that govern the experience of joy found in this psalm. The words of David remind us of Christ's loving submission to his Father: 'LORD, you have assigned me my portion and my cup' (verse 5, NIV). In the Garden of Gethsemane Jesus prayed, 'My Father, if it be possible, let this cup pass from me; nevertheless, not as I will, but as you will' (*Matt.* 26:39). A most dreadful ordeal lay before him. Soon he would face the full fury of man's cruelty, and the wrath of God for the sins of his people. Yet he prays, 'Not as I will, but as you will.' Hebrews 12:2 suggests that when Jesus submitted to God's will, his Father filled him with spiritual joy. Jesus, 'for the joy that was set before him endured the cross, despising the shame.'

Our crosses do not compare to his, but they are crosses still, and they require the same sustaining grace that supported Jesus in his sufferings. Bearing our crosses, we share in the fellowship

[2] D. Martyn Lloyd-Jones, *The Sermon on the Mount* (Grand Rapids: Eerdmans, 1959), vol. 1, p. 75.

of Christ's sufferings; yet in those very sufferings we can also anticipate the joy of Christ's resurrection. Through our trials, Christ teaches us to speak like the psalmist, 'Lord, you have assigned me my portion and my cup; therefore, it is for my good, and my lot is secure in your sovereign will. The place to which you have brought me is pleasant if you are there. If I have you, Lord, I have everything I need.' Jesus knew, even at the cross, that God was sovereignly in control, that his Father was loving and good, that his purposes would never fail. For these reasons, Jesus was able to worship and rejoice.

If any event proves that God is in control even in the darkest hour, then it is the resurrection of Jesus. This is what both David and Jesus foresaw with joy, and Psalm 16 contains one of the great resurrection prophecies of the Old Testament. Peter pointed this out in his Pentecost sermon, using the words of this very psalm. He said that David 'foresaw and spoke about the resurrection of the Christ, that he was not abandoned to Hades, nor did his flesh see corruption' (*Acts* 2:31). The explicit cause of David's joy was this: that whatever might befall him in this life, death was not the end, the grave was not his final resting place. 'For you will not abandon my soul to Sheol, or let your holy one see corruption.'

The same should be true for us, because Christ's open tomb is the greatest source of joy in all the world. It is by the resurrection that God overwhelms our every fear, wipes away every tear, overturns every injustice, removes every curse, and makes way for the blessing of his love. The resurrection tells us that God will not abandon us to our circumstances, that death and sorrow will not have the final say. Here is a power that broke the bands of death, a strength that meets our every need. It is the light that bursts from Jesus' open tomb that inspired David to say, 'You make known to me the path of life.' And it is with confidence in God's power that we may speak of the glories yet ahead: 'In your presence there is fullness of joy; at your right hand are pleasures for evermore' (verse 11).

The psalm concludes with the resurrection hope. David's path in Psalm 16 is one of a faith that rises up to worship our sovereign, loving God, who responds to that worship by planting an unconquerable joy within the believing, submissive heart. Of this joy the psalmist is sure – and knowing this joy changes everything – 'In your presence there is fullness of joy; at your right hand are pleasures for evermore.'

Jesus, Thou Joy of loving hearts,
  Thou Fount of life, Thou Light of men,
From the best bliss that earth imparts,
  We turn unfilled to Thee again.

Thy truth unchanged hath ever stood;
  Thou savest all that on Thee call;
To them that seek Thee Thou art good,
  To them that find Thee, all in all.

We taste Thee, O Thou living Bread,
  And long to feast upon Thee still;
We drink of Thee, the Fountain-head,
  And thirst our souls from Thee to fill.

Our restless spirits yearn for Thee
  Where'er our changeful lot is cast;
Glad when Thy gracious smile we see;
  Blest, when our faith can hold Thee fast.

O Jesus, ever with us stay:
  Make all our moments calm and bright;
Chase the dark night of sin away:
  Shed o'er our souls Thy holy light.

(Attributed to BERNARD OF CLAIRVAUX, 1091–1153;
translated by RAY PALMER, 1808-87.)

10

THE PSALM OF REPENTANCE
PSALM 51

Have mercy on me, O God, according to your steadfast love;
according to your abundant mercy blot out my transgressions (*Psa.*
51:1).

Certain chapters in the Bible are famous for particular
doctrines or themes. 1 Corinthians chapter 13 is known
as the 'love' chapter, and Hebrews 11 is famous for its portraits
of faith. Psalm 51 is renowned as the classic prayer of
repentance. The superscription tells us that it was written by
David after the prophet Nathan confronted him for his sin of
adultery with Bathsheba. One of God's greatest blessings is the
grace of repentance, and David responded to Nathan by doing
what God calls us to do when confronted with our sins. 'David
said to Nathan, "I have sinned against the LORD"' (*2 Sam.*
12:13). This psalm is believed to contain his prayer of repentance
to God and plea for spiritual renewal.

Repentance could be described as the step-child in the family
of Christian doctrines – neglected, unwanted, and
unappreciated. We are eager to talk about grace, forgiveness,
and other supposedly more positive themes. But to many

Christians repentance is seen as some kind of legalistic require-
ment rather than an indispensable part of the gospel. We must
remember that our Lord Jesus began his ministry on the keynote
of repentance. 'The time is fulfilled,' he said, 'and the kingdom
of God is at hand; repent and believe in the gospel' (*Mark* 1:15).
The *Westminster Confession* says repentance 'is of such necessity
to all sinners that none may expect pardon without it' (xv.3).

Simply put, repentance is turning from sin to God. Repentance
and faith are inseparably joined; Jesus said we must 'repent and
believe'. Sinclair B. Ferguson explains:

> Faith cannot exist where there is no repentance . . . I cannot come
> to Christ in faith without turning from sin in repentance . . . They
> are two sides of the same coin of belonging to Jesus.[1]

Repentance is therefore of great concern to Christians and this
psalm is a most helpful guide. I want us to consider four vital
aspects of repentance as they are taught here: repentance requires
confession of sin; repentance relies on God's mercy; repentance
finds cleansing through Christ's blood; repentance produces new
obedience through the power of the Holy Spirit.

Repentance Requires Confession of Sin

The first thing for us to notice about David's prayer of
repentance is his frank *confession of sin*. The first two verses
speak of his need for forgiveness and cleansing, and in verses
3–4 he explains why:

> For I know my transgressions, and my sin is ever before me.
> Against you, you only, have I sinned and done what is evil in your
> sight, so that you may be justified in your words and blameless in
> your judgment.

This is a classic confession, containing an open admission of
sin and guilt before God. Many a convicted criminal feels sorrow
at being caught. But repentance includes feeling sorrow for the

---

[1] Sinclair B. Ferguson, *The Grace of Repentance* (Wheaton: Crossway,
2000), p. 17.

sin itself and the sinful nature from which the sin sprang. Hugh Martin explains, 'True confession is *taking guilt to ourselves before God*. It is the unreserved acknowledgement of the heinousness of sin, and our consequent, inexcusable ill-desert, our righteous liability to the wrath of God.'[2]

Verses 1–5 provide a neat summary of the Bible's teaching on the different aspects of sin and its nature. David employs three different terms for sin, which reveals the importance he places on the problem of sin. First, sin is *transgressions* (Hebrew, *pesha*) in verses 1 and 3. This means to cross a boundary or to break a rule. This is what Julius Caesar did when he took his army across the river Rubicon; he crossed a forbidden boundary and thus became an outlaw. Likewise, sin is rebellion against God's law. This is something of which we are all guilty. A spiritual understanding of the Ten Commandments will make us realize that, like David, we are rebels, law-breakers, and transgressors.

The second word is *iniquity* (Hebrew, *awon*). This occurs in verse 2, and means *perversion* or *corruption*. As David points out in verse 5, this is something that is part of fallen humanity even from our birth.

Third is the word *sin* (Hebrew, *chattath*), in verses 2 and 3. This means to fall short or miss the mark. David realized that he was not the man he was intended to be. Paul applies this to all of us: 'All have sinned and fall short of the glory of God' (*Rom.* 3:23).

When we talk of confessing our sin, all three of these are involved. We must recognize, as David did, the specific ways we have transgressed God's holy law, manifested corruption and fallen short of God's design. David's concern for his transgression is shown in verse 4, where he admits that it is God's justice he has violated, God's holiness he has offended: 'Against you, you only, have I sinned and done what is evil in your sight.' This is not to deny his sin against people, such as Bathsheba

---

[2] Hugh Martin, *Christ for Us* (Edinburgh: Banner of Truth, 1998), p. 41.

and her husband Uriah. Rather, it shows that what grieves him most of all is the fact that he has sinned against God. He has dishonoured God. He has angered God. God is right to judge him: 'So that you may be justified in your words and blameless in your judgment.' This, above all else, dominates David's sorrow, and the same should be true of our confession of sin.

It is one thing to say, 'Well, I did something I shouldn't have done.' But true repentance says, 'I have offended God. I have broken his law.' Many of us stop short of true repentance because we will not admit our guilt. We shift the blame. We lash out at anyone who accuses us. But David shows that when our sin is discovered – by ourselves or by others – we ought to admit, 'I have sinned against God. He is right to judge me.' True repentance, which leads to restoration, requires such a confession of sin.

We saw that sin includes the idea of depravity and of falling short of God's mark. David confesses this thoroughly. He says, in verse 5, 'Behold, I was brought forth in iniquity, and in sin did my mother conceive me.' The point is, says John Stott, 'If the essence of sin is rebellion, its origin is in our fallen nature.'[3]

This is one of the great biblical texts for the doctrine of original sin. Original sin does not refer to the sinful action of our first parents, Adam and Eve, but rather to the effect of their sin – the fallen state into which our race was plunged and the corruption that is now an inherent characteristic of our nature. The depth of David's confession of sin can be seen by his admission of this very truth about himself. He didn't just happen to sin that one time; this wasn't just some random error. No, sin is a deeply ingrained feature of his humanity. He is a sinner and that is why he sinned. David brings his sin to God, not as a small or fleeting problem that can be easily brushed aside. Rather, he presents sin as a colossal problem brewing within his very nature.

[3] John Stott, *Favorite Psalms: Growing Closer to God* (Grand Rapids: Baker, 2003), p. 55.

You, too, must realize that sin is the great problem of your life. Sin dwells in your nature just as blood flows through your veins. You need a radical solution; you need a thorough cleansing; you need to be born again and renewed. You are unworthy before God, far beneath what he intended and expects. Worse still, sin has made you a law-breaker, and your sin has brought you under God's just condemnation, with no human solution available. If you have a hard time realizing this painful truth, if you are prone to deny your sin, to minimize your guilt, then you should pray for God's Spirit to work conviction of sin within you, just as God sent the prophet Nathan to convict David of his sin.

Repentance Relies on God's Mercy

Conviction of sin is a prerequisite for repentance, in the same way that algebra is a prerequisite for higher mathematics. It is realizing our sin and the shame of our guilt that the Holy Spirit uses, in part, to lead us to repentance. And yet, many people do not proceed from conviction of sin to true repentance because they fail to realize the second thing this psalm teaches, namely, that *repentance relies on God's mercy.*

This is, perhaps, the most important thing for us to know about repentance. People are afraid of the very idea of repentance; it terrorizes their minds, because they think repentance relies on their own works. To them, repentance means moral self-reformation, turning their life around before they can come to God. The problem is that they cannot do this because sin is far too strong for them. Its claws are in their flesh and it has them in a bondage from which they cannot escape. It has, as David realized, corrupted their very nature. Discouraged and disgruntled, they become resentful; they make God out to be the problem rather than the answer, and if they hate their sin they hate him even more for demanding a repentance they cannot perform. This was Martin Luther's experience before he discovered the gospel. He was terrified by the guilt of sin. He confessed his sin regularly; in fact, he exasperated his father confessors by his endless sessions in the confessional booth. Then he would set out to do better, only to find that he could not. He once was asked, 'Martin, don't you love God?' Luther honestly replied, 'Love God? I hate God!' Many, today, are like him.

Notice, then, how David begins this psalm: 'Have mercy on me, O God' (verse 1). This makes all the difference to the convicted sinner. It is the difference between sorrow and joy, between despair and hope, between resentful anger and loving worship of God. Repentance relies not on our works, but on God's mercy. James Montgomery Boice explains:

> Mercy is the sole basis of any approach to God by sinners. We cannot come to God on the basis of his justice; justice strikes us with fear and causes us to hide from him. We are not drawn to God by his wisdom; wisdom does not embolden us, though we stand in awe of it. No more does omniscience, omnipotence, or omnipresence. The only reason we dare come to God and dare hope for a solution to our sin problem is his mercy.[4]

This is the great good news that the Christian gospel proclaims to the world! God is filled with mercy and grace. 'For you, O Lord, are good and forgiving, abounding in steadfast love to all who call upon you' (*Psa.* 86:5). God's mercy is most vividly shown in the ministry of Jesus Christ. Think how often he is seen in the Gospels healing multitudes of people. This is God's mercy for a sick and sinful world. Mark's Gospel tells of a leper, the ultimate symbol of corrupt humanity, coming to Jesus. But falling to his knees, he begged Jesus, 'If you will, you can make me clean.' Mark tells us, 'Moved with pity, [Jesus] stretched out his hand and touched him and said to him, "I will; be clean." And immediately the leprosy left him, and he was made clean' (*Mark* 1:40–42). The heart of Jesus, full of mercy, calls you to come to God, just as you are in all your sin that you might receive the forgiveness of sins.

---

[4] James Montgomery Boice, *Psalms*, 3 vols. (Grand Rapids: Baker, 1996), vol. 2, p. 425.

Sin is far stronger than our strength of will, but it is only the second greatest power in the world. There is a greater power, and on it we must rely – the mighty grace of God extended to sinners who cry to him as David did, 'Have mercy on me, O God!'

The importance of this cannot be over-emphasized. If you want to remove darkness, the only way to do it is to shine a great light. The light that empowers our repentance is the mercy of God. When you see how ready God is to save and cleanse you, then you realize that God is the answer, not the problem. Repentance, therefore, does not mean begrudgingly giving up sins that we love and cherish, but rather seeing our sin as the evil slave-master it truly is and turning in faith to the God of mercy who alone can set us free.

Repentance Finds Cleansing through Christ's Blood

How can it be, you may ask, that a holy God can show mercy to guilty sinners? If God is a righteous judge, and if we have transgressed his law, how can he simply blot out the record of our sins? The answer is found in this psalm; *repentance finds cleansing through Christ's blood.* This is taught in verse 7, where David prays, 'Purge me with hyssop, and I shall be clean; wash me, and I shall be whiter than snow.'

Hyssop was a spongy plant that grew in the crevices of stone walls. Because of its shape and texture it was used as a small brush. In Israel's sacrificial system, hyssop was used to sprinkle the blood of the sacrifice on the one to be cleansed. For example, hyssop was used in the cleansing rite for those who were cured of leprosy. The ritual, in Leviticus 14, involved two live birds. One bird was killed, and the hyssop was dipped in its blood, which was then sprinkled on the leper for his cleansing. This is what David seeks: 'Purge me with hyssop, and I shall be clean.' The rite continued. The second live bird was dipped in the blood and was then released to fly away into the sky. This symbolized the complete removal of sin and guilt. The red stain flew upward until it could no longer be seen and finally went completely away. Psalm 103:12 tells us, 'As far as the east is from the west, so far does he remove our transgressions from us.' The rite concluded with the cleansed leper washing his body and clothes, just as David prayed, 'Wash me, and I shall be whiter than snow.'

This is, of course, a great picture of the atoning work of Jesus Christ. Like the first bird, Jesus was put to death for our sin. He died in our place, bearing our sin and guilt. David prays for sprinkling with sacrificial blood, and when we trust in Christ, his blood is spiritually applied to us so that we are made clean. Jesus has completely removed our guilt, just as the live bird flew away. Jesus washes us clean and clothes us in his perfect righteousness. Therefore, the Apostle John wrote, 'If we confess our sins, he is faithful and just to forgive us our sins and to cleanse us from all unrighteousness' (*1 John* 1:9).

Notice how complete and thorough this cleansing is. David says, 'Wash me, and I shall be whiter than snow.' That is a righteousness of which we can hardly conceive, having so little practical experience of it. But if we come to God through faith in Jesus Christ, this is how we stand before him. John tells us, 'The blood of Jesus, [God's] Son, cleanses us from all sin' (*1 John* 1:7).

Some people find it really hard to admit their sin. But there are others who condemn themselves all too freely. What they find so difficult is to believe that there is something which can cleanse them. But God says that if you come to Christ to be washed clean, his blood will make you, not merely cleaner, but really clean. 'Though your sins are like scarlet, they shall be as white as snow; though they are red like crimson, they shall become like wool' (*Isa.* 1:18).

Have you found this cleansing through Christ's blood? The world is filled with great sinners, people who have offended God in gross and terrible ways. Some have committed murder, or assault, or adultery. Some have been vandals and thieves. Some have lied and slandered, have used their tongues to destroy and sow discord, have cheated, have blasphemed God's own name. Every one of us is guilty of terrible sins like these. We are rebels; we are far short of what God demands, desires, and expects.

For some of us our great need is to realize this: to admit and confess that we have sinned against God and are rightly under condemnation. But others are only too keenly aware of this, and they are being crushed under the great burden of unforgiven sin. If you will but look to Jesus Christ, you will find a God who loved ungodly sinners so much that he sent his one and only Son to bear their guilt and punishment. Through the blood of Christ, you will be made whiter than the snow.

Repentance Produces New Obedience in the Power of the Holy Spirit

The Christian life does not end with forgiveness, but rather begins there. Repentance *leads to new obedience in the power of God's Spirit.* Or to put it differently, repentance includes not just *turning* from sin, but also *walking* with God in holiness. David therefore prays, in verses 10–12: 'Create in me a clean heart, O God, and renew a right spirit within me. Cast me not away from your presence, and take not your Holy Spirit from me. Restore to me the joy of your salvation, and uphold me with a willing spirit.'

On the one hand, this shows us what we lose through sin, the many blessings sin steals from us: purity of heart, steadfastness of spirit, the joy of salvation. On the other hand, these are restored to us through repentance. Repentance is not complete without them; indeed, repentance is not sincere and genuine unless it seeks after a pure heart and a steadfast spirit, gospel joy and godly resolve. Salvation is by grace alone; we do not live a godly life in order to achieve repentance. But the one who receives cleansing by Christ's precious blood, who rejoices at the priceless gift of salvation, genuinely desires to lead an increasingly godly life. He who has been forgiven much loves much. Out of gratitude to God flows a new obedience.

A shining example of this aspect of repentance is found in Zacchaeus, the tax collector from Jericho. Zacchaeus had enriched himself by extortion, robbery, and cheating. When Christ saved him, he voluntarily offered to make restitution to all he had wronged (*Luke* 19:8). He could no longer enjoy possessing the money he had sinfully gained, but instead found new joy in making restitution for his sin and in helping those he had hurt.

David had similar motivations. His sin against Bathsheba had terrible consequences for the life of the nation. David was king, and his bad example reverberated throughout the kingdom. He prays for God's Spirit, therefore, not just for his own spiritual recovery but so that he can be busy undoing some of the harm he had done. In verse 13 he wants to 'teach transgressors your ways', so that 'sinners will return to you.' Verses 14 and 15 tell of his desire to sing praise to God. David wants the Jerusalem he has torn down by his sin to be built up by his godliness; he wants the spiritual life of the nation restored (verses 18 and 19).

Verses 16 and 17 make a vital statement that applies to every sinner who turns to God and now wants to give back to him. David writes, 'For you will not delight in sacrifice, or I would give it; you will not be pleased with a burnt offering. The sacrifices of God are a broken spirit; a broken and contrite heart, O God, you will not despise.' This is an important declaration of what Old Testament religion was really all about. God was never interested in mere rituals but in the heart response of a repentant, God-centred faith. So David wanted to offer God his heart. David's heart was one that was now pierced by the gravity of sin, a heart that now truly understood what sin and salvation are all about, a heart that was pliable in God's hands and sensitive to God's truth.

'The sacrifices of God', he says, 'are a broken spirit; a broken and contrite heart, O God, you will not despise' (verse 17). The same is true today; the highest and best thing we can offer God is a heart that has been broken on account of sin and is responsive to his grace. The proper and appropriate fruit of repentance is nothing less than that.

Repentance: A Way of Life

If you have never experienced the blessings of which this psalm speaks, if you have not been forgiven, and cleansed, and renewed, then you must repent now and turn to God through faith in Jesus Christ. Begin by confessing your sin and coming to God for his mercy.

Yet we are mistaken if we think repentance is only something we do at the start of the Christian life. Nor is repentance only for Christians who have sinned in a particularly bad manner, as David had with Bathsheba. The truth about repentance is what Martin Luther proclaimed as the very first of his famous *Ninety-Five Theses*: 'When our Lord and Master, Jesus Christ, said "repent", he meant that the entire life of believers should be one of repentance.' Luther was arguing against a doctrine of penance that was far from the gospel's teaching on repentance. Penance was little more than saying the 'Our Father' or 'Hail Mary' a few times after leaving the confessional booth, or buying an indulgence. But Luther would argue just as vigorously against a prevailing attitude in our day that sees repentance as an unpleasant necessity to be done once and for all at the beginning of the Christian life. He insisted 'that the entire life of believers should be one of repentance'.

Turning from sin to new obedience is the daily pattern of the Christian's life. Sinclair Ferguson writes

> Repentance is characteristic of the whole life, not the action of a single moment . . . Salvation means we are actually being saved.[5]

Repentance requires confession of sin, it relies on God's mercy, it finds cleansing through Christ's blood, and it produces new obedience through the Holy Spirit. This is to be the believer's daily experience. Let me conclude by working this out in a number of areas.

[5] Ferguson, *Grace of Repentance*, p. 11.

First, there is *worship*. One of the worst things that happens when people fall into sin is that they stop worshipping God. They forget that they can bring their sin to God, who in his great mercy offers to forgive and cleanse them. That is a great problem. But there is also a problem when people come to God for worship, but come without repentance. In many churches today, the corporate confession of sin has been removed so as to avoid making non-Christians feel uncomfortable. But the prayer of confession is an essential ingredient of public as well as private worship.

Psalm 51 tells us how to approach God and depicts the attitude we should have in worship. We should never come to worship as self-righteous people. The way to begin worship is the way David did, saying, 'Have mercy on me, O God' (verse 1). We must worship as sinners, coming to a God of mercy through Christ's cleansing blood.

Repentance also affects the way we *study the Bible* and grow in our understanding of Christian truth. The problem with so many professional theologians is that they do not study the Bible with a penitent mind! How should you approach your Bible to receive God's Word? How should you prepare to hear a sermon? With repentance. Is this not a reason why so many get little or nothing out of the preaching they hear? They sit before the minister with hearts that are neither broken nor contrite. They have already decided what they want to believe and are not prepared to yield to God's Word. We should always approach God's Word by confessing the sinfulness of our own thoughts, and the corruption that keeps us from believing and causes us to dispute the clear teaching of the Word. Then we should ask for God's mercy, plead the cleansing of Christ's blood, and pray for God's help through the illuminating work of his Holy Spirit. Christians, and especially preachers, must approach God's Word with repentance.

Finally, how should you *approach the challenges that face you* daily? With repentant faith. You should receive every trial, every challenge, every opportunity as a sinner, guilty of transgression and worthy only of condemnation. What a cure that is to self-pity! You should then remember God's mercy, his willingness to receive your prayers and to help you. You should offer your works, your ministry, your labour through the cleansing blood of Christ – undaunted by their imperfections and the residue of your sin – asking God to receive your efforts in Christ and to give them his blessing. You should ask God for the Spirit to empower you and bless the work that you offer to him.

If you will do that, then God will do more than just cleanse and forgive you; he will do a lasting spiritual work through you. Notice how David asks God, at the end of his prayer of repentance, to prosper Zion and to build up the walls of Jerusalem, the Lord's holy city. The restoration of the repentant king is connected to blessing for his people. Likewise, it is through the restoration of God's repentant people that God brings his blessing to others, revives his church, and restores worship with which he is well-pleased.

11

SPIRITUAL RECOVERY
PSALM 73

Whom have I in heaven but you? And there is nothing on earth that I desire besides you. My flesh and my heart may fail, but God is the strength of my heart and my portion for ever (*Psa.* 73: 25–26).

Psalm 73 begins with a statement of simple truth: 'Truly God is good to Israel, to those who are pure in heart' (verse 1). There is a parallelism at work here, as is common in Hebrew poetry. The phrase 'Those who are pure in heart' is an amplification of the term 'Israel'. God's true people are those whose hearts have been purified by grace, and to them God is good. That is a simple truth. The rest of this psalm, however, is dedicated to showing how hard it is to believe this truth and to be content in the knowledge of God's goodness.

The author of this psalm, according to the superscription, is Asaph. He was a Levite whom David placed in charge of temple worship in Jerusalem (see *1 Chron.* 16:5,7). He was, therefore, a prominent figure and a deeply spiritual man. Despite these qualifications, Psalm 73 records his descent into discontentment with the providence of God, followed by his spiritual recovery that not only restored him but elevated him to one of the high points of Old Testament spiritual experience.

The Problem of Discontentment

One of the great works of Puritan literature, and one of my own favourite Christian books, is *The Rare Jewel of Christian Contentment* by Jeremiah Burroughs. It is a lengthy reflection on Paul's statement in Philippians 4:11, 'I have learned in whatever situation I am to be content.' Burroughs writes:

> Christian contentment is that sweet, inward, quiet, gracious frame of spirit, which freely submits to and delights in God's wise and fatherly disposal in every condition.[1]

Thomas Watson, another great Puritan preacher, also spoke helpfully about contentment, saying:

> We glorify God, by being contented in that state in which Providence has placed us. We give God the glory of his wisdom, when we rest satisfied with what he carves out to us.[2]

Nonetheless, the fact is that most of us find it hard to be content with the circumstances in which God has placed us. We are often discontented, that is, we are not satisfied with God's provision for our lives. Although we seldom put it in this way, it is really God with whom we are dissatisfied. This is a curious phenomenon, since the Bible not only does not promise us sunny skies and smooth sailing all our days but, quite the opposite, it clearly informs us that as God's people we will be beset with troubles. Peter writes, 'Beloved, do not be surprised at the fiery trial when it comes upon you to test you, as though something strange were happening to you' (*1 Pet.* 4:12). Because we are his children, God gives us trials to strengthen our character and to draw us close to him. Having been told this, it is irrational for us to expect a life free from trouble and difficulty.

Discontented Christians can find themselves in good company when they turn to the Scriptures. The prophet Habakkuk

[1] Jeremiah Burroughs, *The Rare Jewel of Christian Contentment* (1648; repr. London: Banner of Truth, 1964), p. 19.
[2] Thomas Watson, *A Body of Divinity* (1692; repr. London: Banner of Truth, 1958), p. 13.

climbed into his watchtower to await God's justification for the woes he was inflicting on Israel. The prophet Jeremiah was a distinguished complainer. Job, of course, had better grounds than we do for discontentment and he exercised them vigorously. And here in Psalm 73 we have a great man like Asaph saying in verse 2: 'But as for me, my feet had almost stumbled, my steps had nearly slipped.'

The first section of this psalm, from verses 2–15, records his descent into spiritual depression, and it begins the way our experience often begins, with envy towards the ungodly. 'For I was envious of the arrogant,' he says in verse 3.

Asaph marshals an impressive argument for his envy. He begins with two observations that caused him to resent God's ordering of this world's affairs. First, he says, 'I was envious of the arrogant when I saw the prosperity of the wicked' (verse 3). Second, the wicked seem to lead happy and carefree lives: 'For they have no pangs until death; their bodies are fat and sleek. They are not in trouble as others are; they are not stricken like the rest of mankind' (verses 4–5).

We can make similar observations and can be prone to the same kind of resentment. I have heard complaints from women about others who slept around and were rewarded with a husband and children, with a house in the suburbs and all they ever wanted. Meanwhile, they, as Christian women, had refused to compromise sexually and were neglected by men as a result. It happens and it is galling. I know of men who stood by their moral principles at work – and what happened? They lost their jobs, they got passed over for promotion, or they otherwise suffered professionally and financially. What about the cheaters and those who play the game? They were rewarded. They now have the powerful positions, well-appointed offices and big salaries. 'How can this be right?' asks the Christian.

A friend was recently at a hotel that was hosting a convention of pornographers. He told me about the Rolls-Royce limousines that packed the parking lot, the jewellery, and the big fat smiles

on every face. It made him angry. The Bible itself depicts this
same reality. A godly man like Joseph can be sold as a slave and
his father Jacob believes his sons' deceitful cover-up. It is a world
in which righteous Lazarus can become a cripple and live in
misery outside the gates of a pompous rich man who cares
nothing for him. Lazarus just lies there, dogs licking at his sores,
before he finally dies in his poverty (*Luke* 16:19–22).

It is not hard to ask God what kind of world he is in control
of, what kind of justice reigns when these things take place. This
world can seem so unfair, cold, and cruel, at least from our point
of view.

But things get worse. Asaph points out that the wicked exult
in their villainy. 'Therefore pride is their necklace; violence
covers them as a garment . . . They scoff, and speak with malice;
loftily they threaten oppression . . . They say, "How can God
know? Is there knowledge in the Most High?"' (verses 6–11).
They laugh at the righteous; they mock their victims, they boast
in the face of God. But they are not struck down in their sin.
Far from it – they win awards, they garner praise, people fawn
over them, while the righteous are forsaken.

Imagine, for instance, someone who commits a terrible crime
– assault or rape or even murder – and who gets off on a
technicality. Imagine how the victim feels, or how the victim's
parents feel. Then the criminal boasts about what he has done,
he smiles at the victims and taunts them. Perhaps he even
threatens more of the same. He writes a book and it becomes a
best-seller. He laughs about pitiful people who do good and trust
in God. Can there be anything more galling than such a thing
as that? Perhaps this has happened to you and it has left you
embittered, just like Asaph.

Asaph envied the wicked's success; he was disgusted with
God's providential ordering of their affairs. Today such a person
would watch a television show like 'Lifestyles of the Rich and
Famous' and fume over such godless wealth. He would tune
into the Hollywood award shows and be incensed by the money

and glamour of those who revel in debauchery and glorify violence.

If we followed Asaph's course we could even end up grumbling against God. But Psalm 73 warns us not to do that. Envy and anger plunged Asaph into a spiritual pit he had not seen or anticipated.

'Behold, these are the wicked; always at ease, they increase in riches. All in vain have I kept my heart clean and washed my hands in innocence' (verses 12–13). That is his terrible conclusion. He finds himself saying, 'It is not worth serving God. All my religion and faith is foolish if this is the way things are.' This is the blasphemy that worldly people believe, but a man like Asaph ought to have known better. First there was envy and indignation, followed by self-pity, and then he finds himself denying altogether the value of serving God. Now it is Asaph who mocks God; having envied the ungodly he is adopting their image and falling into their sin.

The psalmist says of all this, in verse 2, 'My feet had *almost* stumbled, my steps had *nearly* slipped.' It is interesting to see what it was that first held his foot firm, the foothold on which he found traction and from which he climbed back out from this pit. He tells us what it was in verse 15: 'If I had said, "I will speak thus", I would have betrayed the generation of your children.'

This leads us to believe that Asaph knew how ridiculous his self-pitying attitude was. But it is only concern for the influence he will have on others that checks his free-fall. What value there is in being part of a Christian community! How often, when we are too stubborn or depressed to care about ourselves, it is our love for others, and especially for the weak, that reins us in and makes us speak and act in a godly manner. If we are ever thinking the way Asaph was, we should follow his example. He waited to report his feelings and thoughts until he had worked his way out of the difficulties, until he was first able to say in verse 1: 'Truly God is good to Israel.'

Four Steps to Spiritual Recovery

From here, Asaph begins his climb back to a godly way of thinking. Psalm 73 records four steps in his spiritual recovery, four steps that are now set before us when we too need to escape from self-pity or despair or the many other temptations of discontentment. The first of these appears in verses 16–17: 'When I tried to understand all this, it was oppressive to me *till I entered the sanctuary of God.*'

If there is one thing we should learn from this psalm this is it; here is one of the keys to Christian stability and growth. When we are foundering, when we have lost our sense of balance, when we have started falling because of doubt or discouragement or discontentment, when we can no longer remember why we once were so safe and sound and happy as Christians – what is it that enables us to regain our position? The answer is found in verse 17 – 'I went into the sanctuary of God.' He went into the church; in his case, the tabernacle. What he saw there gave him a perspective he had forgotten. He was confronted with a vision of a mighty, holy, and saving God, and that vision changed his thinking completely.

How important is the place of worship! When I encounter a Christian who has badly fallen it is often the case that he has ceased attending worship or, at least, ceased to really participate in the service of worship. One of the reasons we must be constant in worship is because of what we find there. Let me quote Martyn Lloyd-Jones on this point:

> People who neglect attendance at the house of God are not only being unscriptural – let me put it bluntly – they are fools. My experience in the ministry has taught me that those who are least regular in their attendance are the ones who are most troubled by problems and perplexities . . . It is a very foolish Christian who does not attend the sanctuary of God as often as he possibly can.[3]

---

[3] D. Martyn Lloyd-Jones, *Faith Tried and Triumphant* (Grand Rapids: Baker, 1994), p. 109.

Worship, though directed to God, has an effect upon us. It takes our eyes off ourselves, off the troubles and the confusing matters that preoccupy our minds, and focuses our attention on God. Only then do things come into proper focus. 'I could make no sense of this,' Asaph says. 'I was miserable, confused, bitter. But I went into the sanctuary. I went before God. I stopped accusing him and arguing with him, and simply came before him. And when I saw him again my problems began to resolve themselves. Everything looked different when I looked to him.'

Have you ever experienced this while, for instance, you have prayed? You came to God with your petty anger, your self-pity, and self-absorbed attitude. And as you began to pray you realized how ridiculous, how unholy, how unworthy it all was. You became like Job, who at least had a more understandable reason to question God's providence. But when God spoke from the whirlwind, and demanded, 'Who is this that darkens counsel by words without knowledge?' (*Job* 38:2), Job could only reply, 'I had heard of you by the hearing of the ear, but now my eye sees you; therefore I despise myself, and repent in dust and ashes' (*Job* 42:5–6).

How foolish we can be, how quick to self-pity and depression! So we need to be diligent in our Bible reading, in our study of God's awesome attributes and his great saving works. We need to be regular in prayer. But, especially, we must come often into the sanctuary, and gather with the people of God to worship. These are our only protection against ourselves – against our sin, folly, and weakness.

That was the first step in Asaph's spiritual recovery. He came before God. He entered the sanctuary. It is what you must do when you are falling. Go to church despite your feelings! Do not try to solve your difficulty apart from God, but take it into God's presence. This is where spiritual recovery begins.

Second, verse 17 tells us the immediate affect of this: 'Then I discerned their end.' What happened when Asaph lifted his eyes to God? His perspective changed. His horizons were broadened. Specifically, he noticed something he had forgotten in his angry descent, namely, *the end that awaits the ungodly*. He elaborates, in verses 18–20, 'Truly you set them in slippery places; you make them fall to ruin. How they are destroyed in a moment, swept away utterly by terrors! Like a dream when one awakes, O Lord, when you rouse yourself, you despise them as phantoms.'

He had forgotten about this, just as often we do; but what a difference it makes to our outlook on life. The judgment of God! There is a judgment in the end. Therefore, though the wicked may be carefree and prosperous now, though they may avoid punishment in this world, though they may gloat in their violence and crime, and though they mock God now, there is a judgment they cannot and will not escape. While the rich man in Jesus' parable may have been too self-absorbed to notice the sufferings of righteous Lazarus, the story of the two men did not end at death. The man of God who suffered in life was blessed in death, while the arrogant rich man suffered in torment for his sins. That is the perspective Asaph regained: 'Then I discerned their end.'

I once was on an airplane and, from a couple of rows behind me, heard a lively conversation between a middle-aged man and a young woman. His boisterous voice filled several rows of the plane and most of us gave up trying to read or sleep and settled in for this in-flight talk show. The man pontificated on a number of subjects. He debunked religion as a fraud. He extolled the virtues of his carefree, happy-go-lucky life. Having earlier spoken at length about his wife, he later made a sexual proposition to the younger woman. I felt many things towards this man – but envy was not among them! Certainly, he knew nothing of the kind of struggles that a Christian has – spiritual struggles against the world, the flesh, and the devil. Being at enmity with God he was at peace with the world and with sin. Of course such a person is carefree now! He is a child of this present evil age. Meanwhile the believer, having peace with God, has nothing but conflict in this present life. But none of this made me envy the man on the airplane. Unless he repents and turns to God in faith, how sure and sudden will his fall be into inescapable doom.

I thought this especially as the man laughingly recounted the many ailments arising from his smoking and drinking and carousing, along with the daily round of medicines he needed to keep the party going. I remember this incident clearly because at that moment I was trying to read Psalm 73. There before me were these words: 'Truly you set them in slippery places; you make them fall to ruin' (verse 18). On what a slippery slope this boastful man pranced in his dancing shoes! Verse 20 says, 'Like a dream when one awakes, O Lord, when you rouse yourself, you despise them as phantoms.' Worldly and sinful happiness has no more security or substance than a dream that vanishes when we awake from our sleep. So it is for all boastful sinners. Like a house built on a fault-line, all happiness in sin rests upon the brink of woe.

Do you realize this? Instead of being filled with envy, do you look on the wicked, the mocking and arrogant unbeliever, and pity them for their hollow laughter? Do you mourn over the calamity of their sin? Not being able to speak to the man on the airplane, I prayed for his soul, for him to awake from his dreamy state before it was too late. It is only from a perspective centred on God, from an understanding of life gained from the Bible, that we see things clearly. In such a light, it is simply impossible to envy the ungodly. Instead of complaining about our lot we become more fervent in prayer, more diligent in our witness, more sober in our lives. 'Fret not yourself because of evildoers; be not envious of wrongdoers!' writes David in Psalm 37, 'For they will soon fade like the grass and wither like the green herb' (verses 1–2).

The third step in Asaph's recovery came when he *applied these insights to himself.* Earlier, in his depressed state, he complained about how little he received in return for his righteousness. But now he realizes that everything he is thinking about other people is true of himself: 'When my soul was embittered, when I was pricked in heart, I was brutish and ignorant; I was like a beast towards you' (verses 21–22). If the wicked were foolish and brute beasts before God, the same was true of him in his discontentment with God's providence.

Likewise, it is necessary for our own spiritual well-being that we become aware of our own sin and guilt, of our weakness and unworthiness. I earlier cited frequency in worship as an indicator of spiritual health. But here is another: If we are boastful and arrogant before God we are surely far from him. C. S. Lewis put it this way:

> Whenever we find that our religious life is making us feel that we are good – above all, that we are better than someone else – I think we may be sure that we are being acted on, not by God, but by the devil. The real test of being in the presence of God is that you either forget about yourself altogether or see yourself as a small, dirty object.[4]

That is not morbid self-loathing, but healthy realism about our own sin in the presence of God's holiness. It is borne out in the Bible whenever sinners really are brought to see God. They see themselves as naked and dirty, like Adam and Eve after their sin, needing to be clothed in the righteousness of Christ.

If you are disappointed with God's provision for you, I assure you that you have failed to appreciate your own sin and guilt. Therefore we should endeavour to get a fresh memory of our sin. 'Blessed are the poor in spirit,' Jesus taught, 'for theirs is the kingdom of heaven' (*Matt.* 5:3).

The first step to recovery is to come before God in *worship*. Second, we must realize the *end* that awaits the ungodly, and then, third, notice that this is precisely *what our own sins deserve* too. Now we come to the fourth step of spiritual recovery, which is *a fresh appreciation of the blessings we enjoy* from the

[4] C. S. Lewis, *Mere Christianity* (New York: Macmillan, 1958), p. 111.

unmerited grace of God. It is when Asaph realizes that he himself is among the wicked – that he also deserves judgment and destruction – that he then remembers with joy the blessings he previously despised: 'Nevertheless, I am continually with you; you hold my right hand. You guide me with your counsel, and afterwards you will receive me to glory' (verses 23–24). 'How wonderful it is,' he says, 'that though I have been such a sinner, God is with me nevertheless. He holds me in his hand, he guides me in this life. And in spite of all that I have done, there is glory ahead into which he is safely leading me.'

What is this but the doctrine of salvation by grace alone? This is the teaching of the Bible that tells sinners of the God of amazing grace who has provided a way of salvation. Every one of us is a foolish, brutish beast before God. Our lives in sin are built on the fault line of an approaching doom. But God sent his Son to save us – to fulfil the demands of his law on our behalf and then to bear the punishment of our sins upon the cross. By grace alone he offers us the benefits of this great saving work which we are to receive by faith alone: God 'gave his only Son, that whoever believes in him should not perish but have eternal life' (*John* 3:16).

That same doctrine that offered us salvation in the first place, salvation by grace alone, also preserves the Christian from discontentment. Why are you unhappy? Is it not because you think you deserve something that you are not receiving? That is most certainly the case! But the thing you deserve and do not get is the anger and judgment of God upon your sins. While deserving nothing else from God, you shall receive an inheritance of eternal life through Jesus Christ. Your great spiritual blessings have been purchased at an infinite cost to the God you are so prone to resent.

The psalmist realizes this and it leads him upwards to recovery. God has saved us at the cost of his dear Son's precious blood. He has sent the Holy Spirit into our hearts that we might have fellowship with him. He has given us the light of his Word to guide us, and the sure hope of glory awaits us. How can we possibly complain? How can we harbour discontentment towards such a Saviour? Whatever trials and disappointments we now endure, they come with a promise of 'strength for today, and bright hope for tomorrow'. In this light, we see our troubles as the means God uses to wean us from the idols of this world and to draw our hearts to himself.

My Portion For Ever

It is remarkable that within this psalm we find one of the lowest expressions of unbelief and yet one of the highest expressions of spiritual devotion. Having descended into a black hole of spiritual depression, Asaph uttered his horrible statement: he said, in verse 13, that trusting God is vain. The nadir of unbelief is to say that God doesn't matter, or worse, that God is the One from whom we must escape if we want to be happy.

Exactly opposed to this lie is the great truth that forms the apex of faith. We read of it in verses 25–26. He says that nothing else matters if we only have God. 'Whom have I in heaven but you? And there is nothing on earth that I desire besides you. My flesh and my heart may fail, but God is the strength of my heart and my portion forever.' Both of these statements – one despising God and the other glorifying God – come from the same man in the same psalm; surely this proves the importance of a biblically-shaped mindset. The same man finds himself either in the pit or on the heights, either in hell or in heaven, all depending on the way he allows himself to think.

Verses 25 and 26 are so great that I am almost afraid that trying to expound them will only tarnish them. But it is safe to say that our present happiness cannot be found in anything belonging to this world – not in money, achievement, romance, pleasure. Only God can fill our hearts. If we have him we have all that we really need. How much more must this be true for our eternal destiny?

This much is certain – 'My flesh and my heart may fail.' Indeed, they certainly will. This body I serve and feed and pander is not a ship that will take me safely into harbour. But in all that I lack, in all that this whole world lacks, God abounds. 'God is the strength of my heart and my portion forever.' When I consider this, why would I place anything before my relationship with God? Why should I ever complain if I have him? God is what I really need, and all I really need.

Jeremiah Burrough's book, *The Rare Jewel of Christian Contentment,* comes to the very same conclusion:

> It is not necessary for me to be rich, but it is necessary for me to make my peace with God; it is not necessary that I should live a pleasurable life in this world, but it is absolutely necessary that I should have pardon of my sin; it is not necessary that I should have honour and preferment, but it is necessary that I should have God as my portion, and have my part in Jesus Christ, it is necessary that my soul should be saved in the day of Jesus Christ. The other things are pretty fine indeed, and I should be glad if God would give me them, a fine house, and income, and clothes, and advancement for my wife and children: these are comfortable things, but they are not the necessary things; I may have these and yet perish for ever, but the other is absolutely necessary.[5]

That is quite clearly the position at which the psalmist has arrived. He concludes with a great realization and resolution: 'For behold, those who are far from you shall perish; you put an end to everyone who is unfaithful to you. But for me it is good to be near God; I have made the Lord GOD my refuge, that I may tell of all your works' (verses 27–28).

This is what heaven is – to be with God – and, yet, it is not something for which we need to wait in order to enjoy. It is a present reality! If we sincerely believe this, then we will concern ourselves far less with the things of this world, and far more with the things of God: with our faith, with holiness of

[5] *Rare Jewel*, pp. 92–93.

life, with service to God, and with our witness to the world. And in these things we will find, not merely a present contentment, but a joy that will never end, and a glory that will never fade away.

12

A HEART FOR GOD
PSALM 84

How lovely is your dwelling place, O LORD of hosts! My soul longs, yes, faints for the courts of the LORD; my heart and flesh sing for joy to the living God (*Psa.* 84:1–2).

When he was a boy, the great Welsh preacher, Martyn Lloyd-Jones, was sent to live in a nearby town to attend secondary school. Due to his poor circulation he was made miserable by the frigid temperatures there. 'But,' he later recalled, 'I suffered at the same time from a far greater sickness, and a more painful one, which has remained with me all along life's path – and that was *hiraeth* . . . It is difficult to define *hiraeth*, but to me it means the consciousness of man being out of his home area and that which is dear to him.'[1] This feeling of longing never left Lloyd-Jones. All through life he was conscious of not being in the place to which he really belonged, a place suitable for him to dwell in perfect rest. Centuries earlier, Augustine had explained this in terms of man's relationship to

---

[1] See Iain H. Murray, *D. Martyn Lloyd-Jones: The First Forty Years, 1899–1939* (Edinburgh: Banner of Truth, 1982), pp. 23–4.

God, in the famous prayer from his *Confessions:* 'Thou hast formed us for Thyself, and our hearts are restless till they find rest in Thee.'[2]

In his many years of ministry, Lloyd-Jones came to learn that this problem was not merely his own. He writes:

> Man by nature, man without God, is restless . . . Where can we find peace? Where can we find tranquillity? Where can we find rest and peace of mind and of heart and of spirit? Where can we find the point where all is well and nothing troubles? Where is it? Man cannot find it, he is restless. Why? . . . Man, though he does not know it, was made by God, and he was made in such a way that he is dependent upon God. There is the highest thing in man which can only be satisfied by God. Nothing else can satisfy it.[3]

A Home in God

It is this reality that is expressed so clearly in the 84th Psalm:

> How lovely is your dwelling place, O LORD of hosts! My soul longs, yes, faints for the courts of the LORD; my heart and flesh sing for joy to the living God' (verses 1–2).

The superscription of this psalm says that it was written by the sons of Korah, a clan of the tribe of Levi, the custodians of the temple precincts. It seems the psalmist was experiencing some kind of enforced absence from the tabernacle. Many commentators suggest that he was fleeing with David from the rebellious Absalom. Whatever the circumstances, this psalm expresses the longing of a heart, not merely for the religious rituals of the temple, but for the presence of the God of the temple.

Psalm 84 is organized into three sections set apart by the annotation *Selah*, a musical notation possibly signifying a pause. Each section is defined by a beatitude, a statement of blessing. In the first and third sections the blessing is at the end; in the

---

[2] St Augustine, *The Confessions* (Cambridge: Harvard University Press, 1999), I, p. 3.
[3] D. Martyn Lloyd-Jones, *The Cross* (Wheaton: Crossway, 1986), p. 181.

second section it comes at the beginning. The first of these occurs in verse 4, summarizing the psalm's first point: 'Blessed are those who dwell in your house, ever singing your praise.' In his longing for God, this Levite extols the blessedness of those who have God as their home.

In fine poetic style, the psalmist explains this through his envy for the birds that make their nests in the temple courtyards. He contrasts their experience to his own, saying, 'Even the sparrow finds a home, and the swallow a nest for herself, where she may lay her young, at your altars, O LORD of hosts, my King and my God' (verse 3).

Have you ever noticed how easy it is for birds and animals to find a satisfying home in this world? The creatures are able to have their 'highest aspirations' fulfilled in the things of this present life – food, shelter, companionship. You see a dog resting on a rug, a cat preening in the shade, birds settled in the eves of the temple courts. But not so man! The animals attain a contentment far beyond what humans can get from this world. Surely our restlessness is explained by our spiritual constitution which is suited only for a higher realm than this temporal, earthly one.

This is why the Levite pines for God when he is separated from the Old Testament temple. More than in our present age, the true believer then relied on outward ceremonies, on the building and the ritual of the tabernacle and temple. Left without these things that brought God to him, especially the altar on which the atoning sacrifices were offered, the Levite's heart was bereft. 'My soul longs, yes, faints for the courts of the LORD; my heart and flesh sing for joy to the living God' (verse 2). He, like us, has a God-shaped hole in his heart; he can only be fulfilled by the presence of God.

How few realize this today. All of us are seeking a home. We seek rest and peace, belonging and contentment, satisfaction and joy. Yet ours is an age that seeks these things everywhere but in God. That is why ours is such a restless, dissatisfied generation, despite an unprecedented abundance of wealth and leisure.

Think about the man of the world and his restless progression through life. He seeks excitement in dancing and drinking, in thrills and in sex. But does this satisfy him? No! He finds no home in that, no peace, no fulfilment. So, if he has any depth to him at all, he moves on. He pours himself into his job. He attains to wealth and buys a great house and a prestige car. This, he thinks, will make him happy. But it does not. He takes on a challenge, perhaps to rise to the top of his company, perhaps to climb a great mountain. But when he achieves it he is still restless. It is not enough. So he marries and settles down to family life. But still his heart wanders. His wife begins to worry as she sees that unsettled look in his eye. And well she should!

The years pass and he buys a convertible. He writes a book. He tries a hobby. He has an affair. Perhaps he takes up a cause, becomes politically active. Perhaps he joins a church and takes on religious responsibilities. It doesn't matter what it is, because none of it is big enough for him. (By the way, there are female versions of this same progression!) None of it satisfies the soul. He is still restless; with all that he has there is no peace, no home for his spirit. Why? Because only God is big enough to fill the soul that he created for himself.

You add sin and its deadly effects to all this and you have the brutal restlessness that so defines our times. Isaiah pictured it in a most poignant metaphor, comparing the seething restlessness of the sinful world to the churning of the sea: '"The wicked are like the tossing sea; for it cannot be quiet, and its waters toss up mire and dirt. There is no peace," says my God, "for the wicked"' (*Isa.* 57:20–21). Why not? Because sin brings turmoil and only God provides peace.

Only through trusting in God can a man or woman settle, as a bird does in its nest, with peace and satisfaction and with life's great longing fulfilled. No more restless wanderings are needed because home has been found. 'Thou has formed us for Thyself, and our hearts are restless till they find rest in Thee.'

This is what it means to be a Christian. 'How lovely is your dwelling place, O LORD of hosts!' The Christian has found himself, his identity, his purpose, his home, because he has found it all in God his Saviour.

If you have been a Christian for some time, you may have discovered that, wherever you are in the world, you feel at home in a true church, where the gospel is preached and where there are people who know and serve the Lord Jesus. You can be in a strange city, feeling awkward and out of place, but you go to where God's people are and your heart is at rest. It is almost as if you were at home. Why? Because God is your home. In worship with God's people you are brought into the courts of God. 'Blessed are those who dwell in your house, ever singing your praise!' (verse 4).

The Pilgrim Heart

None of us has achieved our full entry into this rest. Having found God and entered into communion with him, we nonetheless continue seeking after him. We become pilgrims journeying to a distant land that is our final home. It is important for us to realize this tension about our present lives – we have not yet arrived at home, even though our hearts dwell there already. Our home is not in this world but in the next. 'Our citizenship', Paul reminds us, 'is in heaven' (*Phil.* 3:20). This is the idea of the second section of Psalm 84, which begins, 'Blessed are those whose strength is in you, in whose heart are the highways to Zion' (verse 5).

Undoubtedly, the exiled Levite thinks of the regular pilgrimages that led God's people to Jerusalem from every corner of the nation. The Hebrew religious calendar was organized around three great feasts for which all the faithful were to appear before God's temple in Jerusalem. In his mind's eye he can see the streams of worshippers flowing toward Jerusalem. He can hear their songs. He can imagine the refreshing strength that flows into aching legs and feet when the city comes into view above the hills. Blessed are they, he reflects, who seek after God.

This, too, is how the Bible depicts the Christian life. Our home is with God and our homeland is yet ahead. In this, Abraham was the prototype for us of the life of faith. The great description of him in the letter to the Hebrews is meant to be a model for us all: 'By faith he went to live in the land of promise, as in a foreign land, living in tents with Isaac and Jacob, heirs with him of the same promise. For he was looking forward to the city that has foundations, whose designer and builder is God' (*Heb.* 11:9–10).

The psalmist's point is that pilgrim believers are blessed, and in this second section he shows why. First, verse 6 says, 'As they go through the Valley of Baca they make it a place of springs; the early rain also covers it with pools.' *Baca* means weeping. Perhaps the psalmist has in mind a particular place along the trail that was especially difficult for travellers; he knows the pilgrimage involves many hardships and this was an especially difficult place.

When I was in the Army I was once stationed at a post that was very hilly and rugged. The road along which we marched to our training sites included two exceptionally difficult climbs. The soldiers named the first *Misery*, which when ascended led to the base of the second hill, named *Agony*. How well I remember *Misery* and *Agony Hills!* The psalmist likewise thinks of a place he knows, called *Baca*, the valley of tears or sorrow.

The fact is that the Christian life includes such places. The Apostle Peter emphasized this in his first epistle. He said, 'For a little while, if necessary, you have been grieved by various trials, so that the tested genuineness of your faith – more precious than gold that perishes though it is tested by fire – may be found to result in praise and glory and honour at the revelation of Jesus Christ' (*1 Pet.* 1:6–7). God employs trials to test us and to increase our faith.

The writer of Psalm 84 speaks similarly. He says that when those who seek God pass through the vale of tears, '*they* make it a place of springs'. Notice that it is the pilgrims who cause this transformation through the strength they receive from God. 'They make it a place of springs' – this points to the sanctifying influence Christians bring to the sorrows of this world because of their relationship with God.

In one of her books, Susan Hunt tells of a friend named Ruth who was converted to Christianity and soon revealed an intense desire to know God more intimately, for which she fervently prayed. Not long afterward she was diagnosed with an aggressive form of Parkinson's disease. She acknowledged that this was a legitimate way for God to answer her prayer. She explained, 'This is not easy . . . but God's Word holds me together in His hand. Now I know as a fact the truth of 2 Corinthians 12:9: "My grace is sufficient for you, for my power is made perfect in weakness."' At this point Ruth paused, then added, 'I suspect I will know this even more in the months to come.' Over those months, as Ruth progressed from a cane to a walker, and then to a wheelchair, before finally taking to the bed on which she would die, she gave constant testimony to a growing knowledge of God that made her Valley of Baca a place of springs. She found that God was faithful, sending, as the psalmist writes, early rains that covered it with pools of blessing and comfort.[4]

Elizabeth Prentiss was another woman who experienced this redemptive transformation in sorrow. In her case, it was her trials that made her tenderly sensitive to the needs of others. In the light of her ill health, chronic insomnia, and the death of a child, her husband wrote, 'Her faith never failed; she glorified God in the midst of it all; she thanked her Lord and Master for "taking her in hand" . . . What is especially noteworthy, her own suffering, instead of paralysing . . . active sympathy with

[4] Susan Hunt, *The True Woman* (Wheaton: Crossway, 1997), p. 88.

the sorrows and trials of others, had just the contrary effect.'
Out of her own tears came springs of mercy for others. To
another woman who had lost a child, Prentiss wrote, 'My dear
friend, don't let this great tragedy of sorrow fail to do everything
for you . . . The intent of sorrow is to toss us on to God's
promises.'[5]

'Blessed are those . . . in whose heart are the highways to Zion,'
says the psalm. 'As they go through the Valley of Baca, they
make it a place of springs.' This does not trivialize our trials
and sorrows. Rather, it tells us why it is only the pilgrim heart
that finds such blessing in a world like ours. It is not those who
trudge along miserably who are blessed. Rather, it is those who
have the pilgrim spirit, and who have the highway to Zion, not
merely under their feet, but in their heart. Their passion is to
press forward in the knowledge of God, to gain more and greater
possession of heavenly things, and to draw nearer to the vision
of God's shining city.

It is this desire for God that transforms sorrows into blessing,
because in our sorrows God makes his love wonderful to us.
Alexander Maclaren writes, 'If we have in our hearts, as our
chief aim, the desire to get closer to God, then our sorrows and
our tears will become sources of refreshment and fertility. Ah!
how different all our troubles, large and little, look when we
take as our great aim in life . . . that we should be moulded into
His likeness and enriched by the possession of Himself . . . The
secret of turning the desert into abundance, and tears into
blessings, lies in having the pilgrim's heart.'[6]

Verse 7 contains the second reason the pilgrim heart is blessed:
'They go from strength to strength; each one appears before
God in Zion.' I want to apply this especially to the weary
Christian, burdened by besetting sins and who looks upon the
life of faith as a long and almost hopeless journey. You may be

[5] Ibid., p. 92–3.
[6] Alexander Maclaren, *Expositions of Holy Scripture,* 17 vols. (Grand
Rapids: Baker, 1982), vol. 4, pp. 134–5.

in the grip of sin, entrenched in the ways of the world, frail in spirit, and discouraged by your weakness. If all did depend on your strength, then the pilgrimage would be without hope. But the psalmist says to God, 'Blessed are those whose strength is in you' (verse 5). Therefore, if you undertake God's journey of faith you will be blessed. Why can you be sure of this? Because your strength is not in yourself but in God. Trust, then, in his promises and look to his Word; fix your eyes on the cross that declares his love toward you and that he has taken away your sin, and you will 'go from strength to strength', until at last you too, like so many before you, will appear before God in the heavenly Zion. The pilgrim heart is not only one that seeks God, but one that looks to him to provide all that is needed, to supply strength for the weak, to keep the straying on course, to lift up the downcast, and restore the fallen.

Are you experiencing this blessing? Are you growing stronger on the way? Are you moving past former sins? Are you engaged in new discoveries of God? Do you know a strength that was not yours before? If not it can only be because the highway that is under your feet is not in your heart, and because you are seeking only worldly pleasures, which he has withheld so that you may be drawn to heavenly glories instead. Only God can fill our souls and only he can give strength to our hearts; if we seek him we will surely be satisfied and filled. 'Blessed are those whose strength is in you, in whose heart are the highways to Zion.'

Lessons along the Way of Faith

Psalm 84 expresses a longing for God, because the psalmist knows that those who dwell in him and seek him with a pilgrim's heart are blessed. The third section concludes with a final beatitude that sums up the whole: 'O LORD of hosts, blessed is the one who trusts in you!' (verse 12).

In this last section, the psalmist relates lessons he has learned along the pathway of faith. He begins with the importance of prayer: 'O LORD God of hosts, hear my prayer; give ear, O God of Jacob!' (verse 8). By example, he shows that the pilgrim heart is strengthened by prayer. Those who seek God pray often. They realize that God is near, that he looks upon his children and is always ready to hear their cries for help.

This specific prayer probably throws light on the psalmist's circumstances. He asks God to 'look on the face of your anointed'. Many scholars say this is a reference to the king, perhaps even to David, with whom the Levite was in exile. This harmonizes with the description of him as 'our shield'. This tells us the psalmist was not alone. He was in company with the Lord's anointed, the king, to whom God had made great promises.

The word *anointed* is in Hebrew *Messiah*; reading this, the Christian cannot help but think of Jesus Christ. Just as the psalmist drew comfort from David's company, and was assured of God's favour, so we can look to our fellowship with Christ, in whose company we walk as his disciples. We pray confidently in his name: 'Behold our shield, O God; look on the face of your anointed!' We know that, whatever our circumstances, we are not alone. Jesus says, 'I will not leave you as orphans . . . Because I live, you also will live' (*John* 14:18–19). Christ is the guarantee of God's covenant favour toward us. He is the Good Shepherd of his flock.

Verses 8 and 9 show that Christian pilgrims have access to God in prayer and that they walk in fellowship with God's anointed, their shield and king. Verse 10 adds a third lesson: 'For a day in your courts is better than a thousand elsewhere. I would rather be a doorkeeper in the house of my God than dwell in the tents of wickedness.' He has learned that the meanest godly service is better than the greatest worldly acclaim; the smallest act rendered to God is far greater than the pleasures of unbelief and sin.

How slow we are to learn this lesson! Have you learned it? Or are you still ashamed of being identified with Christ and his people for fear that you will lose the esteem of the wicked? What a shame it is that the best of us know so little of the spirituality expressed in this psalm. We scarcely, if ever, rise to the heights of this psalmist's fervent spirit: 'How lovely is your dwelling place, O LORD of hosts! My soul longs, yes, faints for the courts of the LORD; my heart and flesh sing for joy to the living God . . . For a day in your courts is better than a thousand elsewhere. I would rather be a doorkeeper in the house of my God than dwell in the tents of wickedness' (*Psa.* 84:1–2, 10).

This pure expression of devotion makes us realize what sin is really about. Sin is not just breaking a few rules. Sin is our failure to rejoice in God in this fashion. The world knows nothing of this adoration and gives God no glory. That is its great sin and condemnation. Many claim to be 'pretty good people', when in fact they are ingrates and rebels.

Christians are not much better. Like the Pharisees, we clean up our act a little bit, we come to church, we do a few good deeds, and we think we have attained to God's standard. All the while our hearts never approach this kind of love for God. At a profound level this is our sin – that we do not render to God the glory he deserves, we do not give him the first place in our lives. We do not pant for the living God, but esteem the pleasures and treasures of this dying world. How great, then, is our constant need of God's forgiving mercy – no less now than when we first believed – and also of the Spirit's regenerating power. May God grant that we, like the psalmist, might learn this lesson, esteeming one day in God's courts better than a thousand in the palaces of this wicked world.

This is the very grace God provides to those who seek it. Verse 11 adds, 'For the LORD God is a sun and shield; the LORD bestows favour and honour. No good thing does he withhold from those who walk uprightly.' This is the only time in the Bible that God is directly compared to the sun, no doubt because of the idea of pilgrimage. To know God in this way is like walking under shining skies, with a bright sun lighting your way and cheerfully warming your heart. He is a sun and shield, providing us with blessing and protection.

Furthermore, 'the LORD bestows favour and honour' (verse 11). This is, literally, 'grace and glory'. These are things the world can never offer, and blessings which the worldly man cannot merit. Nothing we do could ever earn it, but God gives grace to his pilgrim people. The forgiveness we need, the love for which we long, the strength without which we would fail – God gives such grace to those who trust him. What is more, he gives glory. While worldly men and women sell themselves for entertainment, for tawdry measures of success, for riches and power and fame – all of which are fleeting at best and often enslaving – God gives glory to those who seek him. In this life it is the increasing glory of a Christlike character; in the life to come it is the ultimate glory, when we will see him face to face.

'No good thing does he withhold from those who walk uprightly' (verse 11). Yes, the Lord withholds many things, but none that are ultimately for our good. So it is for all who trust him with integrity and sincerity. If we earnestly seek to find our home in God and are walking out from this world and into the next (albeit with faltering steps), we will receive the wise and loving care of Almighty God. Nothing that is for our good will he withhold.

For these reasons, with all that he has learned, the psalmist says, 'O LORD of hosts, blessed is the one who trusts in you!' (verse 12). Have you learned something of that? If you have made your home in God, if you have followed him in the strength he supplies, you too will enjoy this blessedness, this spiritual enjoyment that comes from relying upon God.

'I Am the Way'

In the last meeting before his arrest and crucifixion, Jesus Christ spoke to his disciples about the life of pilgrimage. He told them that he was going ahead of them to God's house, where he was going to prepare a home for them, and that they should follow. When Thomas asked how they could know the way, Jesus replied, 'I am the way and the truth and the life. No one comes to the Father except through me' (*John* 14:6).

In Christ's words is found the answer to every question raised by Psalm 84: 'I am the way.' We have said that the only home suitable for the human soul is found in God. But how, you may ask, do I know God? How do I find him? How do I gain his acceptance? The answer is Jesus Christ. He is the way. It is Jesus who reveals God to the world. It is Jesus whose blood takes away our sin, his righteousness that clothes us so that we might stand in God's holy presence. It is Jesus who opens the door to our home in the heavenly courts of God.

The same is true about the Christian life as a present pilgrimage. Jesus is the way. We start at his cross and finish at his resurrection. As his disciples and sheep we can be sure of God's protection and help. The writer of the letter to the Hebrews exhorts his readers, 'Let us run with endurance the race that is set before us, looking to Jesus, the founder and perfecter of our faith' (*Heb.* 12:1–2).

It is because of Jesus that those who trust in God are blessed. We find in him everything we need, but, especially, as verse 11 says, 'he bestows grace and glory'. This is our *present* – grace from God through the cross – and this is our *future* destiny in Christ – we shall have glory through his resurrection. John says in his first epistle, 'When he appears we shall be like him, because we shall see him as he is' (*1 John* 3:2).

Do you want to love God like this psalmist? Jesus Christ is the way. We love him because he first loved us. He has removed the barrier of our sin so we feel God's warmth like the sun, we know his favour like golden rays of light. Our future with him is glory. For all his troubles, Job praised God because of Christ. 'I know that my Redeemer lives,' he cried, 'and at the last he will stand upon the earth. And after my skin has been thus destroyed, yet in my flesh I shall see God, whom I shall see for myself, and my eyes shall behold, and not another. My heart faints within me!' (*Job* 19:25–27).

If that does not make you long for God then nothing ever will. From strength to strength, God's people advance towards his heavenly city. And as we draw near, and the vision grows brighter, our hearts likewise shall say, 'How lovely is your dwelling place, O LORD of hosts! . . . Blessed is the one who trusts in you!'

13

GIVE THANKS TO THE LORD
PSALM 107

Oh give thanks to the LORD, for he is good, for his steadfast love endures for ever! Let the redeemed of the LORD say so (*Psa.* 107: 1–2).

T his chapter concludes our lessons on the subject of discipleship which we have gleaned from the Book of Psalms. We have seen the psalmist in worship and at prayer. We have considered the joy, peace, and hope that come to those who walk with God. We have seen the psalmist conquering fear with faith, gaining a foothold when he was falling, and being restored to God through repentance. An excellent way to conclude our study is with Psalm 107, which reminds us that the great end of our salvation is that God should be praised for his grace to us. 'Oh give thanks to the LORD, for he is good,' the psalmist begins, 'for his steadfast love endures for ever! Let the redeemed of the LORD say so . . .'

Scholars surmise that Psalm 107 was written to help the people of Israel praise God after their restoration from the Babylonian exile. Verse 3 especially suggests this, since it speaks of a regathering of God's people from every direction. The psalm has three sections: an *initial call to give praise to God* (verses 1–3), a *recounting of the many perils* from which God has saved his people (verses 4–32), and a *concluding statement about God's sovereignty* over all the affairs of men (verses 33–43).

Give Thanks to the Lord

How should we respond to God's wonderful saving grace? The answer is by giving thanks to him. The Christian life has been rightly summarized as *guilt, grace,* and *gratitude.* We come to God *guilty* of sin and enslaved by it; God saves us by his *grace* alone, and as we realize this our response is increasingly dominated by *gratitude.* Here is the great principle taught in this psalm, as Martyn Lloyd-Jones puts it:

> The fundamental note of Christianity, and therefore the chief characteristic of the Christian, is the giving of thanks unto God.[1]

Therefore, a sure indication of our spiritual condition is whether we are often complaining about the troubles we experience and about all the ways we think God has let us down, or if we are filled with thanksgiving for the salvation he has provided at so great a cost to himself.

Psalm 107 reminds us that our lives ought to proclaim the message that the Lord is good and that his love endures for ever. Indeed, this proclamation must be the hallmark of God's people. We are used to identifying people by their associations, by their appearances, by their professed beliefs. But according to the Bible, the true mark of the Christian is evidence of God's grace in the life. The Christian is the one who is joyful even in trials, who has peace amidst the storms, and who can thank God in all situations (1 Thess. 5:18).

Four Pictures of Redemption

Such thanksgiving is the goal of Psalm 107 and the writer seeks to reach it by describing the various ways in which God's saving

[1] D. Martyn Lloyd-Jones, *True Happiness* (Wheaton: Crossway, 1999), p. 86.

grace has come to his people. The main body of the psalm, from verse 4 to verse 32, offers four vivid portrayals of man's lost condition, from which we have been saved by God's grace. The psalmist is assembling a great choir to sing God's praise. This choir is made up of people who have been saved from all kinds of perils, and who now blend their voices together to offer this one song of thanksgiving. This is what the church should be, not merely various kinds of people coming together, but people who each have their own story of salvation to tell, and who mingle their voices harmoniously together in their praise and thanksgiving to God.

The first of these pictures, in verses 4 to 9, speaks of *those who have lost their way in a wilderness:* 'Some wandered in desert wastes, finding no way to a city to dwell in; hungry and thirsty, their soul fainted within them.'

It is not clear which Jewish experience these verses have in mind. Is it a backward look to the Exodus, when Israel wandered through the great desert? Or is this the experience of those who fled from the great catastrophe of the conquest of Jerusalem in 586 BC? Others, and I think this is the most likely view, see this as a general summary of what the exiles had to go through in their return to the land of Israel. Whatever way we think of this, there are abundant biblical examples of God's people needing to be rescued from desert wanderings, and of God providing food and drink to those who were in distress.

This is, however, an appropriate picture of the deliverance Christians have experienced. We, too, have gone astray in sin and have experienced the terrible barrenness that such a life produces. We have been lost in a wilderness, unable to find our way home, with no rest for our souls. We were hungry and thirsty, our lives spiritually ebbing away. Nothing we tried could secure us against the realities of failure, disease, misfortune, and death. All of these things loomed large in our minds, creating a great anxiety. We were like those without a city in which to dwell secure. We were like aimless wanderers lost in a barren land.

Is that not a true picture of life without God? Is that not a life we have known, in service to sin? Taken to its natural end, life without God produces only despair; it is a life without answers to our deepest, most serious questions. There is nothing satisfying awaiting us at the end of life. Do you notice how often the world's great men and women devote their later years to writing their autobiographies and erecting other monuments to the past? Do they do this because they have nothing left except the past? They have no future to which to look forward. Their life has no destination, except the cold, lifeless grave. The best they can do is reminisce about their former glories. They are at the end and there is nothing to look forward to, nothing to get excited about. But for the Christian the future is gloriously bright! The Christian does not live in the past. For the Christian, to live is Christ and to die is gain. That is why a Christian does not only care about his past achievements and former glories; the best is yet to come! The destination is far, far better than the journey. Unlike the unbelieving man and woman, the believer in Jesus has found his way to the city of peace and joy.

Even before the end, the unbelieving life becomes barren. In chapter 2 we noted how Charles Darwin, the 'father of evolution', turned his back on God and committed himself to 'science' and reason. As he grew older, he admitted that he lost his taste for life; no longer could he get anything out of poetry, music, or art. The life of sin, of humanistic logic, is barren; it offers nothing to drink, nothing to feed the soul. Sin shrinks the soul and destroys the man. Lloyd-Jones says:

> Life without Christ is utterly hopeless. There is no way, no path, no life, no truth. It is a wilderness, a solitary way, and it leaves us helpless, hopeless, lost, hungry, thirsty, and with our souls fainting within us.[2]

But God offers salvation to the lost. The psalmist writes,

> Then they cried to the LORD in their trouble, and he delivered them from their distress. He led them by a straight way till they reached

[2] *True Happiness*, p. 110.

a city to dwell in. Let them thank the LORD for his steadfast love, for his wondrous works to the children of men! For he satisfies the longing soul, and the hungry soul he fills with good things (verses 6–9).

What a cause this is for thanksgiving to God! He makes a home, a life, and a way to glory for all those who call upon him. Christianity is not merely a way to get into heaven after you die. It is the way to the experience of fullness in this present life, the way to be spiritually fed and sustained along the way. You see why it is such a tragedy when Christians give the impression that the godly life is sad and dreary. The psalmist is right; he says God 'satisfies the longing soul, and the hungry soul he fills with good things.' Let us therefore live with gratitude to the Lord, 'for he is good; his steadfast love endures forever.'

The second picture of salvation occurs in verses 10–16.

Some sat in darkness and in the shadow of death, prisoners in affliction and in irons, for they had rebelled against the words of God, and spurned the counsel of the Most High. So he bowed their hearts down with hard labour; they fell down, with none to help (verses 10–12).

Here, the problem is *bondage, the slavery that is the product of sin*. How ironic this statement is, because the world makes exactly the opposite claim. People say Christianity is something that weighs you down with chains. True freedom is found by being a man or woman of the world. It is only when you reject God that you can experience true freedom!

This is the lie for which so many people reject their religious upbringing. When they were young they had to go to church, and their parents would not give them the freedom to do all the 'exciting' things that other young people were free to do. But now they have grown up and are no longer under the control of their parents; they have cast off all those old restrictions and now they are free! They can do whatever they want; without God they have liberty.

'Reject God and you will be free' is the first lie the devil told. He whispered to Eve that God was keeping her back from her true potential. When you eat of the forbidden fruit, he told her, when you disregard God's commandments and seize control of your own life, then 'your eyes will be opened, and you will be like God' (*Gen.* 3:5). But that is a lie, and the sordid history of our human race proves it. Verses 11 and 12 explain, 'They had rebelled against the words of God, and spurned the counsel of the Most High. So he bowed their hearts down with hard labour; they fell down, with none to help.'

Sin is rebellion; it is doing our own will instead of God's. It produces bondage; it wraps us in chains so that we cannot live as we ought. We think sin is our servant; we think we can dabble in a godless life-style and have a little bit of fun. But the opposite is the case. Sin is not our servant; it is our master – and a cruel master at that. We find that we cannot stop sinning once we have started. It weakens our willpower, warps our character, and destroys our relationships so that we cannot know the blessings of honour, dignity, truth, and love.

But there is a way out of this bondage. The psalm continues:

Then they cried to the LORD in their trouble, and he delivered them from their distress. He brought them out of darkness and the shadow of death, and burst their bonds apart. Let them thank the LORD for his steadfast love, for his wondrous works to the children of men! For he shatters the doors of bronze and cuts in two the bars of iron (verses 13–16).

God breaks the power of sin. He sent his only Son to die in our place, to bear our guilt to free us from sin's penalty. He sends the Holy Spirit to overthrow sin's corrupting influence in our lives. These are bars of strongest iron, but God cuts through them with the gospel. Charles Wesley sings of this with joy:

> Long my imprisoned spirit lay
>   Fast bound in sin and nature's night;
> Thine eye diffused a quick'ning ray;
>   I woke, the dungeon flamed with light;

My chains fell off, my heart was free;
I rose, went forth, and followed Thee.

Do you want to be free? True freedom is found in knowing God, in serving God, in receiving God's blessing and fulfilling the purpose for which you were made. Salvation frees us to have a relationship with God and to live a godly life. Jesus said, 'If you abide in my word, you are truly my disciples, and you will know the truth, and the truth will set you free' (*John* 8:31–32). Let us give thanks to the Lord who sets the captives free.

The psalm's third picture comes in verses 17–22 where our predicament is seen as *a terrible sickness that threatens to destroy us:*

Some were fools through their sinful ways, and because of their iniquities suffered affliction; they loathed any kind of food, and they drew near to the gates of death (verses 17–18).

Notice that this sickness is caused by the folly of our rebellious ways. This is vividly shown today. People give themselves over to sin, especially sexual sin, and they contract awful diseases for which we have no cure. The AIDS epidemic has exposed sin's destructive power. Certainly, there are people who suffer from this terrible disease through no fault of their own. But in many cases, AIDS is a disease that afflicts those who have given themselves over to sin. If you want to avoid contracting AIDS through sexual activity, you need only practise sexual purity. You need only practise chastity before and faithfulness within marriage. Many are those whose lives have been destroyed by AIDS who thought they could safely give themselves over to sin. We should have compassion on those with such a dreadful disease and minister to them with the love of God. But we should also recognize this true picture of what sin really does – it corrupts us and leads to death.

AIDS is not the only way sin leads to sickness. Sin corrupts our whole being. We were made to be whole, to have integrity, to be pure. But through sin our minds are diseased. Our hearts are sick, with all sorts of perverse and evil desires. This is not the result of chance or fate, but of man's folly in sin.

The good news is that Jesus came as the Great Physician. Think of all the people he miraculously healed during his earthly ministry. His miracles of healing all kinds of sicknesses and diseases provide us with a powerful illustration of what he can do for the soul. He makes us whole and clean and well:

> They cried to the LORD in their trouble, and he delivered them from their distress. He sent out his word and healed them, and delivered them from their destruction. Let them thank the LORD for his steadfast love, for his wondrous works to the children of men! (verses 19–21).

Fourth, and finally, verses 23–32 speak of *the perilous nature of life:*

> Some went down to the sea in ships, doing business on the great waters; they saw the deeds of the LORD, his wondrous works in the deep. For he commanded and raised the stormy wind, which lifted up the waves of the sea. They mounted up to heaven; they went down to the depths; their courage melted away in their evil plight; they reeled and staggered like drunken men and were at their wits' end (verses 23–27).

This is one of the passages that proves how profound is the psychology of the Bible. If you want to really understand life, you should read God's Word. What this tells us is that life is like a voyage. It starts out so well, with such hope and promise. This is how we are in our youth. The sun is shining; the sky is blue and cloudless. We are fit, full of optimism and energy; we are going to conquer the world. But as we begin to live we learn that God opposes the pride of man. We learn this at work when promotions pass us by. We learn this in financial matters; the stock market unexpectedly falls, damaging our savings and pension provision. We learn this with our health. People we know and love die; we find ourselves attending funeral services more often. Perhaps we are stunned by a health crisis of our own. Our strength begins to wane and life becomes a struggle. It happens in our relationships. Friends who invited us to their wedding get divorced. We tell ourselves it could never happen to us, but then our spouse starts showing that absent, distant look. This is the life without God. After just a little while the clouds have rolled in and the sea has become rough. We are tossed high up on the waves and cast down deep into the troughs. As the psalmist says, our courage melts away; our grand expectations have to be lowered. We will be happy just to ride out the storm. The tempest strikes and our anxiety soars. That is the story of many a life that began with arrogant pride: 'They reeled and staggered like drunken men and were at their wits' end.'

Think of the story of the *Titanic* – a tragic illustration of unbelieving man in his overweening pride. It was the 'unsinkable' ship; it set sail with unprecedented fanfare. Oh, the pride and the boasting! But the unsinkable ship never made it to the harbour. The ocean contained unforeseen perils; and so it is for all of us on life's voyage.

The same is true of nations. Martyn Lloyd-Jones says this about the Britain of his youth, just before the cataclysm of World War I:

> In the early months of 1914 the sea had never been smoother. The prosperity of Great Britain had never been so great. The whole world was advancing; it was in a marvellous condition. The British were settling down to enjoy themselves on the sundeck of life. And suddenly something happened in the little country of Serbia, World War I came, and the billows were rising upon England, and we were shaking and rocking in a great convulsion in mid-ocean.[3]

I have wondered of late if the same will some day be said of these years of our own prosperity; is Western Civilization on the brink of another great war, a great catastrophe, a tragic fall, that no-one can foresee? We thought ourselves 'merchants on

---

[3] *True Happiness*, p. 154.

the mighty waters' (verse 23, NIV), but we were in reality on the brink of a terrible and destructive storm.

This, according to the Bible, is what happens in life. But our psalm also speaks of God's saving presence:

> Then they cried to the LORD in their trouble, and he delivered them from their distress. He made the storm be still, and the waves of the sea were hushed. Then they were glad that the waters were quiet, and he brought them to their desired haven (verses 28–30).

The great illustration of this work of God is Jesus standing in the boat among his fearful disciples, stilling the wind and the waves with his bare command. The disciples were sinking, their boat was foundering, but Jesus was with them and he made their journey safe. 'Peace! Be still!' he called. 'Then the wind died down and it was completely calm.' This is what Christians may know, no matter what the storm, no matter how great the peril, that Jesus is with us to give us peace in the storm and to guide us safe to the heavenly shore.

These, then, are four pictures of life without God: *the trackless desert, the dark prison, the deadly disease,* and *the perilous sea.* But the lesson to be learned here is not merely to see what we are saved *from*, but to grasp what we are saved *for*. This is why Christianity makes all the difference. Christianity is not just believing certain things and professing a certain creed. It is a life with God, a blessed life of communion with him. It is what we have depicted here, despite the troubles of this life. Christianity is finding your way and walking a straight path with a glorious destination in view. It is walking with God who strengthens your soul with spiritual food and drink, as you progress toward the 'city that has foundations' (*Heb.* 11:10). Christianity is God breaking the chains of sin with his gospel. It means being healed and made whole again by the grace of Christ. It is experiencing peace and even joy in the storms of this life.

These are the blessings of the gospel of Jesus Christ that we are to believe and receive. Oh, how God will be glorified in our lives as others perceive the difference his presence makes, and as we respond with songs of thanksgiving. 'Let them thank the LORD' – that is the psalmist's conclusion – 'for his steadfast love, for his wondrous works to the children of men! Let them extol him in the congregation of the people, and praise him in the assembly of the elders' (verses 31–32).

God's Sovereignty over Mankind

The psalm concludes with verses that warn us against presumption, and press upon us the moral principles with which God rules the world. Verses 33–34 tell us that the troubles of this life are under God's sovereign control:

> He turns rivers into a desert, springs of water into thirsty ground, a fruitful land into a salty waste, because of the evil of its inhabitants.

This reminds us that it is always God with whom we have to do, and that sin is the ultimate cause of all our troubles with him. Sin is the ultimate cause of all the pain, suffering, and chaos in this world. If we are committed to sin we must expect, both as individuals and as nations, that the God of holiness will oppose us, and that we will feel his reproof. Presumptuously people sing of God's certain blessing, but we have no reason to expect his blessing unless we turn from our sin.

If we want to escape God's opposition and know the joy of his blessing, we need only be cleansed from our sins and restored to his service – the very thing he offers to everyone through Jesus Christ. Those who turn to God, who in faith call on his name and seek to do his will have solid grounds for hope.

Verses 35–38 depict vividly what God is able and willing to do for those who return to him in faith:

> He turns a desert into pools of water, a parched land into springs of water. And there he lets the hungry dwell, and they establish a city to live in; they sow fields and plant vineyards and get a fruitful yield. By his blessing they multiply greatly, and he does not let their livestock diminish.

But when we receive God's blessing we must not turn away from him. We must not give our hearts to idols without expecting God to chastise us and judge us again. Oh, that we might learn the lessons of the history of Israel in the Old Testament Scriptures (*1 Cor.* 10:6)!

> When they are diminished and brought low through oppression, evil, and sorrow, he pours contempt on princes and makes them wander in trackless wastes; but he raises up the needy out of affliction and makes their families like flocks (verses 39–41).

God is unchanging in his rule. He blesses the godly and sends curses on sin. Always it is God with whom we have to do; always it is sin on the one hand or faithfulness on the other that determines how we will fare under his rule.

Let the Redeemed Say So

The psalm concludes:

> The upright see it and are glad, and all wickedness shuts its mouth. Whoever is wise, let him attend to these things; let them consider the steadfast love of the LORD (verses 42–43).

This introduces the first of four applications I would like briefly to draw. The first lesson we should learn if we are to profit from Scripture history and from our own experience is that *we must cultivate a great reverence for God* in all things.

I remember attending a memorial service for a Christian man who all his life had been poor. Though he was employed doing menial jobs, he was rich in wisdom and in the Spirit of God. In the eulogies of his family, one of his grandsons, wrote, 'I remember that he usually said, "Before you do anything, put God first."'

That is what reverence for God is: putting God first. A man who gives that kind of advice has learned a thing or two in life. Psalm 34:9 says, 'Fear the LORD, you his saints, for those who fear him have no lack!' This man's blessed life had been a testimony to that truth from God's Word.

Second, this Psalm teaches us *an eternal perspective on life.* We are going to have ups and downs. We are going to go through barren places. But if we walk with God we know that ultimately there are eternal blessings in store for us. We are going to struggle with sin, but we can, nevertheless, look forward to the day when the fight will be over, when in glory the Lord will strike off every vestige of sin, even as the angel struck off Peter's chains to free him from prison. We will become sick, we will pass through storms, but our Lord will not let us fail. Jesus said it is the Father's will 'that everyone who looks on the Son and believes in him should have eternal life, and I will raise him up on the last day' (*John* 6:40).

Third, this Psalm teaches that *the key to life, the key to blessing and safety, is found in repentance and faith.* As we saw in our study of Psalm 51, this is the way of the whole Christian life – turning from sin and turning to God. That is what we find in each of these pictures of trouble: 'Then they cried out to the LORD in their trouble, and he delivered them from their distress' (verses 6, 13, 19, 28).

If you want to find the good way, if you want to be set free from sin's bondage, if you want to be healed and rescued from great danger, then you must call on God, repenting of sin and turning to him in faith. If you are too proud to call on God, if you will not admit the guilt of your sin and the predicament into which it has led you, if you will not confess your weakness and need, then you cannot be saved. But if you come to Jesus Christ, asking for forgiveness and cleansing, for leading and help, then you will walk with God in the light of his favour. Paul says, 'Everyone who calls on the name of the Lord will be saved' (*Rom.* 10:13).

That leads to my final observation. This psalm exhorts *all who know the grace of God to be thankful:* 'Let the redeemed of the LORD say so . . . Let them thank the LORD . . .' That is what we are to do, and we have every reason to do it; every believer has a great story to tell about the marvellous love of the Lord. He has redeemed us from the hand of the enemy. 'He satisfies the longing soul, and the hungry soul he fills with good things' (verse 9). 'He shatters the doors of bronze and cuts in two the bars of iron' (verse 16). He calms the storm and leads us to safety (verse 29).

This is what God does for all those who trust in him. That is what God will do for any who will call upon his name. But how will the world ever know, unless we, who have experienced this amazing grace, give thanks for the greatness of his steadfast love, unless we declare his praises with thanks-giving and with thanks-living?

Let us make it our business as we walk with God to remember the fullness of our blessings in Christ, not only to appreciate what we are saved *from* but to take hold of all that we are saved *to*, and then to fashion our lives into a living witness, so that others may enter into this life of thanksgiving and praise.

Let them offer sacrifices of thanksgiving, and tell of his deeds in songs of joy! (verse 22).

DISCUSSION QUESTIONS

Psalm 1: The Way of Blessing

1. What do we mean by 'communion with God'? What are the obstacles that keep us from it?

2. How does Psalm 1 depict the progression of the sinful life? Why should we be so careful about the 'counsel' that our minds receive?

3. The author states, 'The way of blessing begins with the Word of God.' How does this line up with the statement of this psalm? What advice would you give a new believer about studying the Bible?

4. Verse 3 paints one of the great descriptions of the blessed Christian life. Discuss it. Is this a realistic possibility for people today? What kind of prosperity does the psalm have in mind?

5. Can you think of anyone whose life fits the description of verse 3? Are there any examples in the Bible?

6. Verse 4 describes the wicked as 'chaff'. What is chaff? Is this a fair description of the unbelieving life?

7. How is Jesus a perfect example of the 'blessed man' of Psalm 1? Why is his blessing a source of hope to us?

Psalm 8: What Is Man?

1. What is a 'worldview'? Why is it important? What four questions and answers determine our worldview?

2. What does Psalm 8 say about who and what we are?

3. What does it mean to live a life filled with wonder? Where does wonder come from?

4. Why is humility a valuable indicator of our relationship with God? Why is it important to God that we be humble?

5. What is the source of mankind's dignity? How does this help us to turn away from sin and turn upwards towards God?

6. How is Jesus Christ the answer to the question, 'What is man?' How can we become more like Jesus, so that our lives proclaim, 'O LORD, our Lord, how majestic is your name'?

Psalm 23: My Lord, My Shepherd

1. Christians often speak of enjoying a personal relationship with God. How does the statement of verse 1 help you to envision your relationship to God and his to you?

2. Have you ever interacted with sheep? What were they like? What does this description convey about us?

3. Psalm 23 says that God will provide for his sheep. What three things are described in verses 2–3 as God's provision for us? Are you aware of having received these from God?

4. How does knowing, 'I shall not want,' help us to follow God 'in paths of righteousness'?

5. Are you surprised to learn that the path of righteousness leads through dangerous valleys? In verse 4, why should we not be afraid in the presence of trials and dangers, and even death?

6. Can one of God's sheep be sure that he 'shall dwell in the house of the LORD forever?' If so, what is the Christian's confidence that he will endure to the end?

7. How did Jesus Christ apply the teaching of Psalm 23 to himself? How does this Psalm strengthen our faith and inspire our love for him?

Psalm 121: I Lift Up My Eyes

1. Psalm 121 begins, 'I lift up my eyes to the hills. From where does my help come?' Discuss. What do you think of as the 'hills' to which we lift our eyes?

2. In what sense is it right to seek human sources of help? What are their limits? Can we rely on them in the end?

3. What makes God such a great helper? What are some of the attributes of God, and how do they encourage us about his ability to help us in our needs?

4. Why is Psalm 121 so dear to pilgrims? What key statement does it make about God's care for his people?

5. The author reminds us of Jacob as an example of one who learned about God's guardian care for his people. Can you think of other biblical examples?

6. 'This psalm does not promise us an absence of troubles, but rather assumes them.' What comfort does it then offer us? How has God proved the claims of this psalm through Jesus Christ?

7. How should the message of Psalm 121 influence our prayers? How does it help us encourage believers who are tempted to lose hope? What statement does it make about the believer's hope in death?

Psalm 103: *How to Praise the Lord (Part One)*

1. Have you ever felt that God has let you down? What caused you to feel that way? How would you biblically evaluate that attitude?

2. What is the relationship between head religion and heart religion? How is it depicted in the opening verses of this psalm? What does this suggest for your spiritual life?

3. The author states that 'only those who remember their sins will really praise the Lord with thanksgiving.' Why is that?

4. David next speaks of the healing of our spiritual diseases and our redemption from the dark pit of misery. How might you remember these so as to praise the Lord?

5. David says that God 'satisfies you with good' (verse 5). With so much material abundance, why aren't people satisfied today? With what satisfactions are believers blessed?

6. David concludes his list of blessings with the Christian's inward renewal. How have you experienced renewal after a time of weakness? What caused your faith to sprout wings again? What provides God's people with strength and vigour like the eagle's?

7. Discuss the testimony of Corrie ten Boom. Compare her story to the spiritual blessings David speaks about in verses 3–5. How did she respond to them so as to honour God with praise?

8. Do you find it difficult to forgive? What enabled Corrie to forgive her former prison guard? What does this teach you about forgiveness?

Psalm 103: *How to Praise the Lord (Part Two)*

1. Have you ever loved someone without respecting them? Or have you ever respected someone without loving them? Why are both of these needed for a balanced Christian life?

2. How does David prove God's love for his people? To what do we look for an even greater proof of God's love? How does this stir us up to love the Lord?

3.   How is it that 'God does not deal with us according to our sins?' How can God be just and yet forgive us? What is the extent or the measure of his forgiveness?

4.   David illustrates God's love by comparing it to that of a father for his children. What was it about your earthly father's love that is so important to you? If our human fathers have let us down, how can we turn to God to love us as a true Father?

5.   The author suggests that perhaps our greatest need today is the recovery of awe for the glory and majesty of God. Do you have a strong sense of awe toward God? How would its recovery transform your worship and your life?

6.   The psalm links our worship to our witness. What is the connection between the two? Looking back over this whole psalm, where does it speak most powerfully to you?

Psalm 5: How to Pray

1.   Do you find it easy or hard to pray? Do you think your prayer life is an area of strength or of weakness? Why? How does your flesh war against your spirit in prayer?

2.   Verses 1–2 tell us that prayer is coming to God. What descriptions does David use for prayer in these verses? How do you experience these?

3.   Verse 3 suggests that we ought to arrange our prayers before we begin. How might you practise this to strengthen your prayer life? What sorts of things should we 'arrange' before we go to God in prayer?

4.   David said of his prayer, 'I watch'. Why is that so important? What reasons do we have to be confident about prayer? Why does expectancy in prayer lead to persistence?

5.   According to the author, what ought to be our chief aim in prayer? About what things should we praise our Lord?

6.   What makes prayer 'work'? Do we have to 'get prayer right'? When we read that David looked to God's 'holy temple', where does that encourage us to look for confidence in our prayers? Read 1 Peter 3:18. How does this encourage you?

7.   Verses 11–12 indicate that prayer is important for our possession of spiritual joy. How does David experience this in these verses? Do you know someone who especially possesses joy because of prayer? What have you learned from them?

Psalm 56: *From Fear to Faith*

1.   What sorts of things do you fear? What effect does fear have upon your spiritual life?

2.   The author says that fear leads us to 'take matters into our own hands'. What is often the problem with doing that? How might prayer have helped David, and how might it help us in times of danger or trial?

3.   Discuss the title of J. B. Phillips' book, *Your God Is Too Small*, as it relates to the problem of fear. In what ways is our idea of God often too small? What does the Bible tell us about God that assures us that he is 'big enough' for all our needs?

4.   In verse 10, David suggests that his faith comes from God's Word. Can you think of any portions of the Bible that especially encourage you to trust in God? How important is regular Bible study to a life of faith instead of fear?

5.   Earlier, we discussed sources of fear in this world. Now, having trusted God anew, David says, 'What can flesh do to me?' In the light of God's attributes and his promises in the Bible, how do we answer that now?

6.   Edward Welch states that whatever we fear will always control us. Have you experienced this? What is the difference between 'fear of man' and 'fear of God'?

7.   Verses 8–9 suggest the role of prayer in David's recovery of faith. Why must you be regular in prayer if you are to be led by faith instead of by fear?

Psalm 16: *Pathway to Joy*

1.   Contrast common ideas about happiness with the biblical idea of joy. Why is joy 'one of the clearest signs of communion with God?'

2.   What enables Christians to have joy even in difficult circumstances? Why is it so important that we do? What is the first step that David takes in pursuit of joy?

3.   In verses 2–4, the author suggests that David is taking a 'spiritual inventory', so as to gain a God-centred perspective on his life. What does he mean? How might we do this?

4.   Read verses 5–6 again. What strikes you about this statement? How is faith necessary for us to attain this kind of submission to God's will? What is the value of it?

5.   How does David's attitude differ from a 'cold, resentful submission'? Why does he 'bless the Lord' in the midst of his trials? Why should you?

6.   Martyn Lloyd-Jones writes, 'They alone are truly happy who are seeking to be righteous.' What does he mean? Is this true? Why? Support your answer biblically.

7.   What enabled Jesus to submit to God's will on the cross? How was his resurrection proof that his trust in God was well placed? How does the resurrection serve to encourage you to submit to God with joy?

8.   Reflect upon the closing words of this psalm: 'In your presence there is fullness of joy; at your right hand are pleasures forevermore.'

Psalm 51: The Psalm of Repentance

1.   Why is repentance the 'step-child' in the family of Christian doctrines? How are repentance and faith related?

2.   In verses 1–3, David defines sin using three terms. What are the terms and what do they say about sin? How do each of these shape the way we ought to confess our sins?

3.   What does the doctrine of original sin teach? How does verse 5 support this doctrine? Why is this important for us to understand and believe?

4.   Have you found it difficult to repent? Why is it so important to realize that repentance relies upon God's mercy? How is mercy the light that chases away the darkness of our sin?

5.   When David prayed, 'Cleanse me with hyssop,' what did he mean? How is it that repentance finds cleansing? What does it mean to us when David says, 'Wash me, and I shall be whiter than snow'? (v. 7). Explain this in terms of 1 John 1:9.

6.   Read verses 10–12. What blessings do we forfeit when we sin? How can these be restored to us through repentance?

7.   Why is new obedience essential to true repentance? What do we learn about this from Zacchaeus' repentance?

8.   What does it mean that the whole life of a believer is one of repentance? How does repentance shape our approach to worship? To Bible study? To the daily challenges of life?

Psalm 73: *Spiritual Recovery*

1. How might we define Christian contentment? Why is contentment so difficult for us to learn?

2. Asaph was discontented because of his envy for the ungodly. Have you ever felt that way? Why? What were Asaph's specific grievances? What was the effect on his spiritual life?

3. Psalm 73 describes spiritual recovery in four steps. The first is, 'I entered the sanctuary of God.' Why is consistent attendance in worship so important for our spiritual stability? What is it about being in the house of God for worship that helps us to recover spiritually?

4. What was Asaph's second step to spiritual recovery? (see verse 17). What did he realize about the 'end of the ungodly?' Do you ever think about the fate that awaits all who have turned from God? How should that change our attitude towards them and towards our own lives?

5. Asaph next considered his own sin, realizing that what was true about others was also true about him. What is it that can keep us from hypocrisy and self-righteousness? What helps you to be humble and contrite before the Lord? What is the importance of this to our spiritual health?

6. What is the fourth and final step of spiritual recovery depicted in this psalm (verses 23–24)? Does the doctrine of salvation by grace alone have practical value for our spiritual health? How?

7. Where did Asaph's spiritual recovery bring him, as described in verses 25–26? Why does the author call this 'one of the highest expressions of spiritual devotion'?

Psalm 84: *A Heart for God*

1. What does Augustine's famous prayer mean? What is its importance for our lives?

2. What is the message of verses 1–4? Why does the psalmist envy the birds who nest in the temple? Why is it that without God, we are all restless in this life? What is the remedy for this?

3. Verse 6 says that pilgrim believers are blessed because 'they make the Valley of Baca a place of springs.' What does this mean? Have you ever experienced this in your own life or seen it in another's? How does this challenge us about our attitude towards trials and sorrows?

4. The psalmist speaks of those 'in whose heart are the highways to Zion'. How do we cultivate a pilgrim-heart?

5. What does this psalm say about the necessity of prayer in the life of a Christian pilgrim. How does prayer function in this psalm (verses 8–9)? How might you strengthen your walk through a more biblical attitude towards prayer?

6. Is verse 10 the regular attitude of your heart? If not, what is keeping you from thinking and speaking this way? What does it reveal to us about the true nature of sin?

7. Jesus said, 'I am the way' (*John* 14:6). How is he the way to finding our home in God? How is he the way to gaining a true pilgrim's heart? And how is Jesus the way for us to be blessed as those who trust in the Lord?

Psalm 107: Give Thanks to the Lord

1. Have you ever felt especially grateful to another person? How did it affect your relationship with him or her? Why is gratitude such an important part of our relationship to God?

2. The first picture of redemption deals with those who have lost their way in a desert waste. How does this depict life without God? What kind of salvation does God offer (verses 6–9)?

3. What condition is depicted in verses 10–16. ? What great lie does the author confront through this picture? Have you ever fallen prey to it? How does God deliver those in bondage to sin?

4. The third picture speaks of sin as a terrible sickness (verses17–22). Can you think of any gospel accounts in which Jesus healed people who were sick? How do you have cause to give thanks to God for his healing grace in your life?

5. The fourth picture shows 'the perilous nature of life' (verses 23–32). Is life really this dangerous? What experiences have you had that awoke you to the perils of this present world? How are we to be saved if life is so dangerous?

6. How does Psalm 107 depict repentance as essential to our salvation? What blessings do we receive through repentance and faith, as depicted here?

7. As you reflected on this psalm, and especially on the four portraits of redemption, what stirred you to a renewed sense of thanksgiving to God? How might this thanksgiving help you to honour God in new ways?